Can God be trusted? This is the question R
Assured. Rachel empowers her readers to ur
making theological distinctives accessible, in.
This message has the power to draw us closer to Christ, deepen our faith, and increase
thoughtful meditation on Scripture.

KAT ARMSTRONG
Bible teacher and author of *The In-Between Place: Where Jesus Changes Our Story* and the
6-book Bible study series Storyline Bible Studies

Rachel Booth Smith has the exquisite gift of weaving together stories that span genera-
tions in order to illuminate the Great Story, the one that begins and ends all other stories,
the Story that sets us free. Booth Smith is equal parts scholar, sister, and compatriot. Her
voice untangles, enriches, and inspires. Perfect for both personal growth and rich discussion, *Rest Assured* unleashed in me a new awe of the God who is restoring all things.

KIMBERLY STUART
Author of *Star for Jesus (And Other Jobs I Quit)*

In a world that often feels like chaos, Rachel offers a fresh perspective of rest. Her accessible
deep dive into ancient Near East cultures gives insight to the rest offered in the one true
God and adds a dimension of admiration and trust to our worship. In a moment of com-
motion, Rachel's words feel like the wise friend who puts her hand on your shoulder and
reminds you to breathe deeply and look to the Creator. This book is a gift, and I'm thrilled
that Rachel's words are now available for more hands to hold.

MONICA RITCHIE
Christian podcast and radio host

Rest Assured is just what your mind and heart have been searching for in this restless world.
Rachel delivers deep theological insight with the approachability of an everyday person
living through everyday struggles. A must-read for all believers who are searching for rest.

MEREDITH BROCK
CEO of Proverbs 31 Ministries

Thoroughly researched and beautifully written, Smith has made scholarship accessible to
those who need it the most: an often restless and anxious church, which dearly needs this
beautiful reintroduction to the God revealed in early Genesis. Her work is a true gift in
that regard, masterfully guiding the reader through the discovery process, yet with a gentle enough touch for those who may have some unlearning to do before true learning can
begin. Smith is a true scholar of the Scriptures, and at the same time a brilliant communi-
cator. Both gifts are on display in this book, which I highly recommend to anyone wanting
(or needing) to immerse themselves in the context of early Genesis such that they are better
able to receive the invitation to the Lord's Sabbath rest and rule.

DAN LOWERY
President, Pillar Seminary

This is a delightful little book about a very important topic: finding "rest," a biblical kind of rest found only in trusting, worshiping, and serving God. The author combines serious study of Genesis 1 and related passages of Scripture with wonderful stories from her life and family that illustrate it magnificently. She has a special gift of reading the Bible in its ancient cultural context and explaining it in an understandable way. This volume is well researched and well written. I found it to be not only a joy to read, but a deeply impactful application of the truth of Scripture for the daily lives of people.

RICHARD E. AVERBECK
Professor Emeritus of Old Testament and Semitic Languages, Trinity Evangelical Divinity School

Vividly enter the creation room of God and allow Rachel Smith to carry you on a journey of the creation story like you have never experienced it before. Holding in tension Western and Eastern cultural mores, and Ancient Near East customs, with a splash of Rachel's lived experiences to achieve Sabbath rest, provides a compelling argument of the true meaning of the seventh day of creation. Combining biblical fluency and literacy, the story of creation is masterfully recreated for young and old readers alike. Simply fantastic.

DONNELL J. MOORE
Academic Dean/Professor, Pillar Seminary, and Director of Christian Education, Daytona District/Central Conference – AME Church

If you are looking for a fresh angle, a jump-start for your discipleship to Jesus, *Rest Assured* is the place to turn. Rachel mines the creation story for both spiritually moving and practical ideas that inform, shape, and energize our confidence in God. From the Creator God we gain so much assurance that we can truly rest.

BISHOP TODD HUNTER
Diocese of C4SO (ACNA) and author of *Deep Peace*

Chaos and stress make me want to hold more tightly to my illusion of control. But in *Rest Assured*, Smith reminds me—and you—that our Creator God really does have the whole world in His hands. Through a comprehensive exploration of the creation story, Smith gently draws us to trust confidently in the Lord of the Sabbath.

KELLEY MATHEWS
Coauthor of *40 Questions about Women in Ministry*

Rachel makes Genesis 1 accessible for the average person! She helps us see the creation account through the cultural eyes of the intended audience—the Ancient Near East—and does to in a way that is understandable to the non-theologian. In so doing she answers many questions that most of us have had for years about creation. In addition to helping you feel confident in handling questions about creation, this book will help you to better understand what Sabbath means and why it is God's gift to us.

MIKE SCHATZMAN
Missionary with Cru in Portugal and author of *Expecting Hardship: An Honest Conversation About Missionary Life*

RACHEL BOOTH SMITH

REST
ASSURED

WHAT THE
CREATION STORY
WAS **INTENDED**
TO REVEAL
ABOUT
TRUSTING GOD

MOODY PUBLISHERS
CHICAGO

Unless otherwise indicated, all Scripture quotations are taken from the (NASB®) New American Standard Bible®, Copyright © 1960, 1971, 1977, 1995 by The Lockman Foundation. Used by permission. All rights reserved. lockman.org.

Scripture quotations marked (NLT) are taken from the Holy Bible, New Living Translation, copyright ©1996, 2004, 2015 by Tyndale House Foundation. Used by permission of Tyndale House Publishers, Carol Stream, Illinois 60188. All rights reserved.

Scripture quotations marked (NIV) are taken from the Holy Bible, New International Version®, NIV®. Copyright © 1973, 1978, 1984, 2011 by Biblica, Inc.™ Used by permission of Zondervan. All rights reserved worldwide. www.zondervan.com The "NIV" and "New International Version" are trademarks registered in the United States Patent and Trademark Office by Biblica, Inc.™

Edited by Ashleigh Slater
Interior design: Puckett Smartt
Cover design: Kaylee Lockenour Dunn
Cover image: Cover design of landscape collage copyright © 2023 by nyothep/Adobe Stock (572812702). All rights reserved.
Cover element of setting sun copyright © 2023 by sirins/Adobe Stock (222945381). All rights reserved.
Cover element of starry sky courtesy of Unsplash, Jeremy Perkins.
Author photo: Jennifer Trautmann, Gratitude Photography

Library of Congress Cataloging-in-Publication Data

Names: Booth Smith, Rachel, author.
Title: Rest assured : what the creation story was intended to reveal about trusting God / Rachel Booth Smith.
Description: Chicago, IL : Moody Publishers, [2024] | Includes bibliographical references. | Summary: "We often approach Genesis as a science manual. How did it all happen? But the ancient Israelites were concerned with different questions-questions of purpose . . . who and why. Rachel helps us focus on the who of Creation so we can find meaning and rest for our souls"-- Provided by publisher.
Identifiers: LCCN 2024010882 (print) | LCCN 2024010883 (ebook) | ISBN 9780802432742 (paperback) | ISBN 9780802472762 (ebook)
Subjects: LCSH: Creation--Biblical teaching. | BISAC: RELIGION / Christian Living / General | RELIGION / Christian Living / Spiritual Growth
Classification: LCC BS680.C69 B66 2024 (print) | LCC BS680.C69 (ebook) | DDC 231.7/65--DC23/ENG/20240408
LC record available at https://lccn.loc.gov/2024010882
LC ebook record available at https://lccn.loc.gov/2024010883

Originally delivered by fleets of horse-drawn wagons, the affordable paperbacks from D. L. Moody's publishing house resourced the church and served everyday people. Now, after more than 125 years of publishing and ministry, Moody Publishers' mission remains the same—even if our delivery systems have changed a bit. For more information on other books (and resources) created from a biblical perspective, go to www.moodypublishers.com or write to:

Moody Publishers
820 N. LaSalle Boulevard
Chicago, IL 60610

13579108642

Printed in the United States of America

For Stephen, Clara, and Abbie,
may God grant you the grace to trust Him more and more.
I love you.

CONTENTS

CHAPTER ONE

RESTLESS HEARTS

THIS IS MY FATHER'S WORLD.
O LET ME NE'ER FORGET
THAT THOUGH THE WRONG SEEMS OFT SO STRONG,
GOD IS THE RULER YET.

When my daughter Clara was six, she was diagnosed with cancer. Our reality abruptly shifted within three days.

On Thursday, she was fine. On Friday, she fell and ruptured the tumor. By Saturday, she was an inpatient in the children's hospital cancer ward. After a surgery to remove her tumor-encased kidney, there was a hospital stay, chemo, and radiation. My career as a carpool driver and afternoon snack dispenser ended, and I became a full-time student in the bewildering world of medical acronyms and medication side effects.

One day, Clara and I were driving home from an oncology visit. Sometimes, I would reach my hand back to hers as she sat in her booster chair—and today was one of those days. It had been long hours of appointments, and we were both tired. She was bald and nauseous from the chemo. I was exhausted from playing medical quarterback and keeping an upbeat demeanor, smiling reassuringly to my little girl as nurses administered poison.

We typically rode home in silence with Audrey Assad or Sara Groves playing. Within that Year of Cancer, in an act of sheer grace, both artists had put out albums that directly applied ice to our swollen hearts. Today, as we traveled the highway, Audrey's song "Restless" came on, the chorus repeating a phrase in St. Augustine's *Confessions*:

> I am restless, I'm restless
> 'Til I rest in You, 'til I rest in You
> Oh God, I wanna rest in You.[1]

I heard Clara's quiet voice from the back seat. "Hey, Mom?"
"Yeah?"
She took a deep breath. "Is it a sin to feel restless?"
I paused. Was it? I didn't know. Theologically, I was at a loss. My mom instincts kicked in, and I realized that she needed to know that it was okay to feel the storm of our season.
"No, honey. God knows that sometimes it's hard."
She sighed and stared out the window, singing softly with the tune.
It's been over a decade since that day, yet her question teased my mind for years. *Is it a sin to feel restless?*

REST IN CREATION

Childhood cancer is extreme, but a restless heart can plague any situation. Our emotional equilibrium is fragile, slipping quickly into frustration with one child's shriek, a car breakdown, a work crisis, or an argument with a loved one. As Augustine notes (in his same paragraph about unquiet hearts), we who are humanity "carry our mortality about with us."[2] Our impermanence and infirmities can feel like a threadbare jacket we can't take off.

As we experienced the frailty of our humanity in our home, rest looked like a nice idea rather than an attainable reality. Restlessness rang true. Rest did not. It wasn't until years later that I had the bandwidth to dig deep and explore what rest meant.

After Clara recovered fully from cancer, I started seminary. There, I fell in love with the complexity and texture of the Bible, especially the way God revealed Himself to Israel within their culture and language. I learned that the word *rest* meant something very different to an ancient Israelite than it did to my modern mind. In a class titled Torah, we began our studies with creation. We saw that creation stories were widespread and commonly told, probably around the universal storytelling backdrop: campfires.[3]

Interestingly, I learned rest is the culmination of many ancient Near East (ANE) creation stories, not just Genesis.[4] These stories are like term papers ending with "in conclusion." If the story announced that the deity was at rest, then creation was complete.[5] Additionally, in Genesis, rest wasn't about God taking a nap or saying "whew" as He collapsed into a recliner. In the creation literary styling, rest is best understood as an enthronement or God sitting down on His throne. This enthronement—whether it's in Genesis or an ANE story—only happens after the world has achieved complete harmonious order.[6] When the throne is occupied and the deity rests, the story is complete.

In our modern world, we have a similar concept when making big changes. For instance, what needs to be in place before a significant career change? Do you need your desk set up? Are your financials in order and your healthcare plan in place? Did you finish those online training modules? Once the essential tasks are completed, when you finally sit at your desk ready to take on your new role and rock it—that's rest.

Or how about after a move? The signed purchase or rental agreement doesn't mean it's time to rest. It's still necessary to get the furniture in place, find the elusive forks, set beds up, locate the box labeled "sheets," and finish the seemingly endless to-do list. When all those things are in order—when you can take a breath and start running your home—that's rest.

Rest means that everything is set up just right and running well. In the creation story, we learn that when God is at rest, people can be at rest too. Why? Because all of His creation is just right and running well, and God is on the throne.

A HOLY EAVESDROP

Learning the dimensions of the word *rest* showed me I had been reading the creation story with a very Western mindset. I had to replace my image of God collapsing into a La-Z-Boy[7] (as I have done after a long day of work) with the image of a satisfied Creator reigning over a perfectly designed creation. It turns out that many of my expectations about the ancient text of Genesis were unintentionally infused with my twenty-first-century mindset. Peeling back that mindset and stepping into ancient Israelite sandals took me a lot of time, study, and humility.

In Genesis, we get the privilege of a holy eavesdrop, leaning over the ancient Israelites' shoulders and listening to the truths God shares. Dr. John Walton of Wheaton College notes that "the Bible was written *for* us, but not *to* us."[8] When we read Genesis, we assume that God is introducing Himself to us, but He's not. This introduction is made explicitly to the ancient Israelites, using their language and culture, but knowing that it would be preserved and passed down so that we might benefit from this holy eavesdrop (like Paul's letters to ancient churches in distant lands). We are part of the eventual audience because, as Dr. Walton says, the introduction is *for* us.

Setting aside our natural tendency to read a text as if we are the initial audience is difficult. We slip into assumptions from our own context without even noticing. For instance, it may bother us to read that light was created before the sun. Our inclination is to make a scientific explanation retrofit into the narrative or even to claim this as proof that creation is a fable.

Those two conclusions leapfrog over the first question we should ask: *Would the creation of light before sun bother the intended audience?* If the answer is no, we are asking a modern question that the text is not answering. (Don't worry. You can read more in the section called Twenty-First-Century Questions on p. 173.) When modern assumptions invade our reading, we will almost always get pulled away from what the text is trying to communicate.

One such modern assumption has to do with science. If you've been in the church for a while, you are likely familiar with the issues debated between the science and church communities. Maybe you've been put off by the debate, or perhaps you have a side you've taken. It may seem odd to you, but none of those issues belong in the Genesis creation room.[9] These are all modern concerns, foreign and irrelevant to the ancient Israelite.

All this is to say that science is not going to be a part of our conversation together. Take a deep breath and relax because we aren't going to delve into those issues or the baggage they possess. Together, we will examine the text for the elements it *is* trying to explain. By not reading it as a scientific account, we will discern what it can provide.[10] We are going to read creation as a piece of sacred and true literature, putting ourselves in the shoes of an ancient Israelite as much as we are able. We will listen well to their concerns, learn parts of their culture, and appreciate their understanding of the world.

THE FIRST HELLO

Our task, then, as good Bible readers, is to pay attention to the diverse cultures across the ANE. Who were these ANE men and women? Scholars debate the period that God's people first heard about His creation.[11] What's relevant for our study is that the Israelites who initially encountered the first chapter of Genesis and were part of the ANE cultures would be familiar with commonly shared stories (just as Marvel and Star Wars movies are commonly known today by both superfans and five-year-olds who have never seen the films but can identify Iron Man on a T-shirt). These Israelites had a multicultural heritage (Ex. 12:38; Deut. 26:5) with exposure to varied stories and storytelling from Mesopotamia to Egypt.[12] Across the ANE, people were deeply theological; to them "all experience was religious experience, all law was spiritual in nature, all duties were duties to the gods, all events had deity as their cause."[13] In the view of ancient people, the world came into being because the gods had a purpose for it. All actions were either parallel or counter to that purpose; the natural and supernatural were interrelated.[14]

Just as we are disturbed by restless hearts, so were they. They wanted to know what God cared about, and so do we. A glance at the self-help section of Amazon will tell you we wonder if we have value and purpose, and so did they. They wanted to know their place in the world and how to live, and so do we. Families were very important to them, just as they are to us. They wondered if they would have enough provision, or if relational harmony would ever come easily. Those concerns rank high on our priority list as well. Genesis 1 is intended to answer these questions. We can ask the same questions the ancient Israelites asked and then read the well-written theological literature of creation for God's answers.

Our focus will be on the nature of our Creator and what He intended life to look like in His creation. The way God set up our world to run shows us His priorities.

Did God set up creation to be for His benefit? Were other gods involved in creation? Did He use warfare or diplomacy? All these questions are answered in the first thirty-four verses of Genesis (Gen. 1–2:3), quietly speaking to the ANE cultures and telling them about the character and values of God from the beginning. The answers speak to us too. What an amazing privilege it is to read this introduction.

SACRED LITERATURE

You and I can learn about creation in this way because history, archaeology, and language scholars have all done deep dives into ancient Israelite cultural perspectives and literature. In the coming chapters, I will share ways they have held up their findings to the light and turned the kaleidoscope just a bit, revealing colors and dimensions that are simply stunning.

After I studied how an ancient Israelite would have heard the creation account of Genesis, it was like a black-and-white movie was suddenly in vivid color. The theological implications for God's reign on day seven have given me a direction within my identity as an image of God, revealed God's heart to provide for His creation, and helped me handle tragedy.

To best study creation as twenty-first-century Christians, we will stick close to the original text and context in Genesis. The original context of Genesis includes learning how Israel's contemporaries thought about everyday events (like the sun rising). If we can get a sense of the broader cultures, the contrasts in God's message will naturally be highlighted. Original texts for Israel's neighboring cultures include reading an ancient Egyptian creation story or looking to Mesopotamian writings to learn how they saw the world.

Don't worry. Examining other pieces of ancient literature doesn't mean we will encounter Genesis as fiction. I believe the Genesis creation account is true and absolutely happened. Its beautiful stylings are written using a type of storytelling the ANE person could readily theologically process in a way that holds profound truths about God's character. When we look at creation as *sacred* literature, we can find nuances we may have missed. I want to show you the kaleidoscope of biblical insights within creation. The way God chose to introduce Himself and His character is truly awe-inspiring. Reading this one story well can change how you see God.

In this book, we'll learn how to approach this ancient text written three thousand years ago by checking our expectations and making sure we don't set ourselves up for misunderstanding. Then we will walk together through the days of creation, always focusing on who our God is and how He presented Himself to an ancient culture. Most of all, we will look at what God set up and called "good" before He rested. We will learn that creation calls us to rest, but more than that, it tells us *why* we can rest.

A POSTURE OF REST

Rest is meant to be our daily posture because our soul finds a restful posture anchored in God's character. Day seven persists.

Just as in our earlier example, where the house is running and the job is active, the world is running and God is reigning.

If I could go back and talk to Clara's tender six-year-old heart, I would tell her that being troubled is different from being restless. I would remind her of the truths I have learned in creation: that God set up a beautiful world, put us in it last, loves to be in relationship with us, and a glance at the birds on our drive can remind us that He cares. It is remembering who God is, His value for humanity, His provision, and His beauty that grants our souls rest.

Rest is found in knowing the God of creation. As Augustine notes, "Because you have made us and drawn us to yourself, and our heart is unquiet until it rests in you."[15] But, for a Christian, rest must go deeper than acknowledging God is seated on His throne. Rest is found when we align our restless hearts with *who* God is as He reigns. Together, we will explore the opening verses of history and find God's design is a place of rest.[16]

CHAPTER TWO

MORE THAN A STORY

SUMMER AND WINTER, AND SPRINGTIME AND HARVEST;
SUN, MOON, AND STARS IN THEIR COURSES ABOVE
JOIN WITH ALL NATURE IN MANIFOLD WITNESS
TO THY GREAT FAITHFULNESS, MERCY, AND LOVE.

One Christmas, when I was about six, I remember hearing a
song playing on the television as I lay awake in a sleeping bag at
my grandparents' house. I was supposed to be asleep, but the ex-
citement of the season and traveling to visit family had me wide
awake. I slipped out of my covers and peered into the room where
the adults were watching TV. To my delight, my mom motioned
for me to join her, and I crawled up in her lap.

The Sound of Music was playing. A governess named Maria
sang and danced with seven beautiful children, charmed a strict
naval captain, and then put on a puppet show! The only musicals
I'd seen before it were animated Disney movies. But now, on the
screen, actual adults, not cartoon characters, were bursting out in
song, and I was captivated. It was truly delightful how the film-
makers told a story by weaving together beautiful cinematogra-
phy, tight dialogue, and music.

When I sat with my mom that evening, it would have been

fair for me to expect *The Sound of Music* to operate like every other live-action movie I had seen. But when the nuns started singing about a problem named Maria, I had a choice to make. I could go with it and allow the film to work the way it was designed to, adapting to the idea that musicals can be done by actors, not just cartoons. Or I could refuse to accept that my experience with the genre of musicals was limited. By letting the (still-new-to-me) genre of live-action musicals tell the story with song, I got to discover new dimensions and allow those with the vocal skills to use their gifts.

No one will start singing in Genesis during the creation story. However, as we look closely at Genesis, many of us will encounter a new-to-us style of literature. We all have expectation tripwires when we approach a text, similar to how I expected a live-action movie only to have dialogue. Assumptions we make about what we are reading (or, in my six-year-old case, watching) may set us up for misunderstanding.

A VERY GOOD PLACE TO START

Before we open a book, we usually have an idea about what type of literature we will encounter. Between the call numbers on a library book and the blurbs on back covers, we know if we're settling in for a historical romance, a comedy, self-help, or even searching for cooking tips. If we opened our cookbook and found algebra instruction, we'd certainly be frustrated that the book hadn't met our expectations.

The Bible is so very fun to read because it is full of all sorts of genres, and even mixes them sometimes (like Hannah's poetic prayer in the middle of a narrative about Samuel's birth). Sometimes, there will be different books that are completely different genres that reference the same subject matter. For instance, Psalm 105:1–15 and Genesis 26:1–11 both speak about God confirming His covenant. The Psalms take the long view of Israel's entire history, using poetic phrasing and focusing on God's faithfulness. Genesis points out the specific part of a story, using it to highlight God's faithfulness and landing hard on Isaac's foolishness.

Even though they are both within the Bible, we likely read the psalm and the story in Genesis without having to think about what style is being used. Our experience with a poem or story means we probably don't feel the need to remind ourselves that poetry uses phrasing or that narrative uses a story arc. That familiarity is second nature. But if we are not familiar with the way Genesis 1–2:3 is written, it will take a bit of intentional reorientation to read creation as a unique type of story with its own distinct features.

Approaching the Genesis account of creation is almost universally done as a straightforward story. Every child's Sunday school teacher worth their salt has taught this one as a narrative (I have a particular affinity for the ones who used flannelgraph), and for great reason! It reads similarly to a narrative, and the places it veers off the narrative path and gets a little wonky are easy to sidestep. In fact, for most of my life, I read Genesis as a straightforward story, plugging it into the stylings of every other narrative I read.

Reading creation as a simple narrative that shares facts absolutely serves up the main point that God is Creator. But it wasn't until I began to read it in the style many biblical scholars believe it was written in that I started to grasp the deeper meaning the text was conveying.[1] I learned that a more in-depth read will (in addition to those truths) tell us about *who* the Creator is, why He created, and how knowing His character lets us rest.

Together, we want to grasp these amazing truths, so in the coming chapters, we are going to work hard and listen well as God introduces Himself to the ancient Israelites. To do that, we are going to read creation as a type of story you may have never read outside of Genesis. While it can sometimes look like a simple narrative and has elements of poetry, it is really doing its own unique thing: *cosmogony* (pronounced: koz-*mah*-jon-e).[2] Cosmogony is "an account of how the structured universe came into being."[3] To put it plainly, a cosmogony is a creation story. It has elements of a narrative (like the book of Esther), prose (think "I Have a Dream" by Martin Luther King Jr.), and even poetry (like Walt Whitman). This is a type of story specific to ancient cultures, and in that way is out of print, so to speak. Many of us rarely encounter this style of literature except for the opening pages of our Bibles or in history class. To the ancient Israelites, however, a cosmogony was as familiar as a cookbook is to us.

Reading the first chapters of Genesis as a specific type of sacred literature doesn't mean we are saying it isn't true! The Word of God is true, authoritative, and reliable. Just as the psalmist, the prophet, and the patriarch tell the truth, Genesis is telling us the truth about the God who created heaven and earth. God let the psalmist use his creativity and artistry to communicate, and the account of creation uses the stylings specific to the ANE to make a beautiful introduction to the ancient world.[4]

CREATION JEOPARDY

Literature is shaped by a worldview (poetry by Maya Angelou is much different from poetry by Emily Dickinson). A culture's worldview can help us understand their context, and it can help us understand their literature. One of the important things to note about a cosmogony in the ANE cultures is that it is shaped by a worldview concerned with questions of *purpose*, not questions of *process*.[5]

The diverse ancient cultures were not primarily interested in how the universe came to be, though they were certainly intelligent and curious about many things. They were interested in these kinds of purpose questions:

- Who put everything in place?
- Why did it get ordered this way?
- Why am I here?

You may say, "Hey! We're interested in questions of purpose too!"

Sure. But we often don't match up questions of purpose with a creation story.

As a white woman in the twenty-first century, the questions I have about creation are likely very different from those of an Israelite woman in 1200 BC. If Alex Trebek were to say, "Genesis 1" for Answers in the Bible for $400, I would buzz in and say something like, "*How* was the world made?" My ancient Israelite friend, however, would hit her buzzer and likely say, "*Why* was the world put together this way?" If we aren't careful, we can assume that our questions are the same ones that the ancient Israelite had.

Our two different responses to Creation Jeopardy speak directly to our different worldviews. As we listen in to the introduction God is making to the Israelites, it's important not to buzz in with "How was the world made?" every time we hear God say something about creation.

Learning that the true story of creation was designed to

answer the ancient Israelite's question, "Why was the world made?" or even the question, "Who put everything in place?" has been life-changing for me. It made all the difference when I switched my perspective and began hunting for insights about God's revealed character. The purpose questions the ancient Israelite held are the same ones I hold: *Who is this God who created with a breath? And why did He put it together the way He did?* When I began to see that the first chapter of the Bible held God's plan for how the world was intended to run, it was a game changer.

As we read creation together, we're going to remain mindful of the purpose questions a cosmogony was designed to answer. We will remember that creation was not written *to* us (though it was written *for* us). And as God answers those purpose questions we share with the ancient Israelites, we will learn about His power that can never be lost, His provision that is designed to reproduce in abundance, His definition of order, and His ability to bring order to chaos. What an amazing opening to the Bible!

THE NATURE OF OUR CREATOR

In the coming chapters, we will walk through the days of creation and listen as God speaks to His people. The work of history, archaeology, and linguistics experts will help paint pictures of life and beliefs three thousand years ago. We'll be enlightened and challenged by the way an ancient text can shape our understanding of God and His creation, and getting to know God's character will strengthen our trust in who He is.

We are also going to read cosmogony excerpts from Egypt and Mesopotamia (Babylon, Sumer, and Ugarit)[6] and learn a bit about how they operate (check out the Cosmogony Quick Reference in the back). The more cosmogonies we are exposed to, the better we can understand what was expected and what was unique. So, we will take a look at a few features of cosmogonies that were standard, and then we will watch as God reveals His character by switching things up a bit.

It's a little like how we recognize a Western. Specific features tip off the audience to that style: cowboy hats, a saloon, or a show-down at noon. If we know what's normal to a Western, when something unique or out of the ordinary enters the scene, like a woman sheriff, we'll know when to lean in a little. Learning about cosmogony features will help us know when God is doing some-thing out of the ordinary and teaching the ancient Israelites about His character or how the world was designed to run.

For example, a feature of all cosmogonies is that the deity brings order from chaos. What's different in Genesis is the *way* God brings order: with stated words and blessing, not violence or manipulation. This, among other contrasts, can inform us about God's values and character. After all, getting to know who God is is the point of examining these texts. It's good to believe in God as our Creator; it's a wonder to look at God revealed in creation and say, "I can't imagine anything better than Him. I'm so glad He's in charge."

The greatest introduction ever written awaits us in Genesis. We can read outside of our comfort zone and expectations to find real and meaningful insights about who God is. If you've always assumed that the creation story is a simple retelling of facts (as I had for many years), approaching it as a cosmogony can be a huge mind shift. For me, a little bit of humility was needed to approach a text on its own terms, rather than insisting that it bend to my own.

The first time I watched *The Sound of Music*, I fell in love. And not just with that movie but with musicals in general. As a kid, I watched everything from *West Side Story* to Elvis features. Later in life, I passed this love on to my kids and was proud as punch the day I realized they knew every word in *Singin' in the Rain*. When the musical *Hamilton* came out, with its hip-hop and meshed timelines and cultures, we belted out every lyric in the kitchen while making dinner. For me, adding music to live-action theater made two-dimensional stories 3D. Reading creation as a cosmogony has done the same kind of thing; it's added depth and scope, and it's truly lovely.

Not only is yielding to the text important and fascinating, but it is also honoring the author. By letting the text communicate to us in the way it was designed, we acknowledge that beauty, honesty, and dynamics are at play within its structure. We are admitting that we may need to do a little cross-cultural work. This respect is easily given to Shakespeare, Francis of Assisi, and Bonhoeffer. Let's honor our most exalted book too.

CHAPTER THREE

BEGINNING AT THE END

GENESIS 2:1-3 {DAY SEVEN}

THUS THE HEAVENS AND THE EARTH WERE COMPLETED,
AND ALL THEIR HOSTS. BY THE SEVENTH DAY GOD COMPLETED
HIS WORK WHICH HE HAD DONE, AND HE RESTED ON THE
SEVENTH DAY FROM ALL HIS WORK WHICH HE HAD DONE.
THEN GOD BLESSED THE SEVENTH DAY AND SANCTIFIED IT,
BECAUSE IN IT HE RESTED FROM ALL HIS WORK WHICH GOD
HAD CREATED AND MADE. (GEN. 2:1-3)

When I was four months pregnant with our youngest child, Abbie, we made a short-term move to Tokyo with six-month-old Clara and our two-year-old son Stephen. (Yes, you read that right.) We made the choice to upend our lives and fly across the globe as naïvely confident young adults, excited about travel and opportunities to experience life from a completely different perspective. Even though pregnancy kept me from enjoying the amazing sushi, it was a great time.

What was not so great was the culture shock. Some things were hard (I missed the Clean Air Act in the States as many stores and restaurants were filled with cigarette smoke), and some things were a pleasant surprise (the polite and kind decorum of the people). It was quickly apparent that I wore way too many colors and stuck out like a sore thumb, and my two-and-a-half kids were a bit of an anomaly in downtown Tokyo, where small children were rarely seen. It was not uncommon for elderly women to stop us on the street and try to slip Stephen some candy.

Most mystifying, however, were the maps. We didn't yet have GPS on our phones, so we relied on the folded maps in our pockets and the large ones at the bottom and top of subway stations. I'd wrestle the stroller off the subway car and find a map to orient myself, noting that I needed to walk three blocks up, take a right, and then left. But when I got up to street level, the map was somehow turned! Now it showed that I needed to walk three blocks to the right! How was I to know which way was correct?

It turned out that in Tokyo, maps were oriented toward the direction you were facing as you looked at the map. If you were facing west while figuring out directions at the bottom of the station, then west was at the top. At the street level, if you were facing north when looking at that same map, it was flipped so that north was at the top. I was perpetually lost and confused until I figured out this cultural difference. My American assumption was that all maps had north at the top.

DESTINATION: REST

Often, in our lives, our experiences have drawn the map of our understanding of God's character and how the world was designed to operate. We work from our own viewpoint, as I did when looking at a map in Tokyo. You hold up your map, and I hold up mine, both of us sincerely convinced and maybe sincerely lost.

Creation is the map unmarred by our experiences and by the

sin of the world. When we read the first page of the Bible, we see God's design for how things were supposed to be from the beginning. Since our first breath, we have only known a broken world, but God saved a window for us to view His very good design. Within this opening in Genesis, we see the panorama of perfection, revealing God's definition of order and purpose.

Cosmogonies are a little like peeking at a map of each culture's theology. Each map states, "Here are the instructions for how to interact with the god, and here is how the world was designed to run." The map can then be folded up and handed to humanity when a deity rests in the story because everything is in place. As we see in Genesis, on the last day of creation—day seven—God rested and sat down on His throne. The world was ready to run, turning and functioning as it was intended.

There have been times I've held up the map of my experiences and been disappointed or felt defeated. I've thought, *This is what You put together? No thanks.* God has gently corrected my thinking by showing me the map of the world as it was intended. When the maps are side by side, there are places and experiences on my map that still look like God's intended creation—like the trees that make delicious peaches, the lovely sunsets, the wisdom in the world's design—but when compared closely, I can see where the maps aren't aligned. I've learned that God agrees with the grief on my map, and together, we can say, "This awful thing was not good, and it wasn't a part of the design." Looking closely at God's map of creation, leaning over shoulders at the ANE campsite, and then comparing that map to mine is where the lightbulbs have gone off, and I've grown to trust who God is.

To see those lightbulbs and attempt to hear creation as an ancient listener, let's look at how rest was used in cosmogonies.

We'll start with the Egyptian cosmogony called the "Memphite Theology." Notice when Ptah, an Egyptian deity, rests in this story:

> So has Ptah come to rest after his making everything and every divine speech as well, having given birth to the gods, having made their towns, having founded their nomes, having set the gods in their cult-places, having made sure their bread-offerings, having founded their shrines, having modelled their bodies to what contents them.[1]

Ptah came to rest *after* making everything. Rest here is certainly a ceasing of work but also a reflection that the creation is complete and ready to run. This wasn't indicating that Ptah needed a break but that he was finished.

Other ANE cosmogonies talk about the end of a creation account by stating that the gods are enthroned. In a Sumerian ANE cosmogony, the gods are seated at a banquet in their temple after creation is complete.[2] In another story from Babylon, *Epic of Creation (Enuma Elish)*, the gods are enthroned at a banquet table once there is a well-run and peaceful cosmos.[3] Check out these lines from *Enuma Elish*:

> "We shall lay out the shrine, let us set up its emplacement,
> When we come (to visit you), we shall find rest therein."
> . . .
> All the orders and designs had been made permanent,
> all the gods had divided the stations of heaven and netherworld,
> the fifty great gods took their thrones . . .[4]

Just as worship, communion, and prayer can all indicate a church service, so *enthronement, ceasing work,* and *resting* are all indicators of the same event all across the cultures of the ANE. We can see this is true in Israel too. In Psalm 132, the psalmist uses both rest and enthronement in reference to God's reign:

> For the LORD has chosen Zion,
>> he has desired it for his dwelling, saying,
> "This is my resting place for ever and ever;
>> here I will sit enthroned, for I have desired it."
> (Ps. 132:13–14 NIV)

In their cosmogonies, the gods of Babylon, Egypt, Sumer, and Ugarit all sat down on their thrones when the world was in order. As a part of the literary styling used across Mesopotamia (including Israel), when the gods were enthroned, resting, or stopped work, it signified that creation was complete, and the earth was set up to run the way the deity wanted it to.

SACRED INTRODUCTION

On the seventh day, God set up His reign, declaring that each of the six previous days had been developed perfectly. An examination of those six days against the backdrop of other ANE cosmogonies reveals some startling distinctions about God that have enlarged my understanding of His design.

One such distinction is that Genesis is the only cosmogony to use a seven-day progression. If you've been reading the Bible for a while, you've probably noticed that some numbers come up a lot. Seven is one of those. And it's not limited to just the Scriptures. This particular number also appears in writings across ANE cultures in storytelling and religious activities.[5] Seven days could be used for something as tender as an Egyptian love letter,[6] or as grand as a Babylonian priestess installation.[7] In both scenarios, they indicate something is unique or lovely, making the lady's heart flutter or the ceremony majestic. If something is seven days, it is special, so take note.

Israel's was an ANE culture, so seven was important to them as well. When God is added to the seven equation, special quickly upgrades to sacred. The Bible uses seven years to build the temple (1 Kings 6:38) and seven days (times two) to dedicate it (1 Kings 8:65–66; Ezek. 45:21–25; 2 Chron. 7:8–9). The purification ritual for a man with leprosy to enter the community with God's people was seven days (Lev. 14:8–9). Seven times around Jericho on the seventh day meant God's people could watch God have a miraculous victory (Josh. 6:1–20).

Scripture clearly links the number seven to the sacred. But what did the word *sacred* mean in Israel and the broader ANE cultures? It was not every day with an added sprinkle of holy water; rather, it indicated something set apart requiring rituals, prayers, and sacrifices to enter. Sacred often denoted the presence of the god. In Israel, Mesopotamia, and Egypt, trespassing on a sacred space was egregious, invoking severe punishment. It would have been impossible for a temple to be dedicated without significant ceremonial activities; a priest wouldn't dream of entering the temple space without the appropriate consecration. Israel had similar stipulations—one could not simply walk into the meeting place of God and men (2 Chron. 26:16–23).

These rituals were big deals, much more than simply praying over an event. They took days, and involved fasting, shaving heads, separation from family and friends, and ceremonies. Many people were involved, and very specific instructions were carried out.

Western Christians don't really have a metric for this. We

regard most things casually, even religious matters. We throw around the word *sacred*, and the word *holy* mostly precedes a curse word. Our casual attitudes aren't necessarily a problem, but it does mean we don't quite grasp the gravity of an ancient person's association with those terms.

When creation in Genesis finished at the seven-day mark, it set off the sacred alarm bells in the ANE reader's head. This would have been universally understood as a big deal around the campfire. God was not engaged in a regular activity or just playing around when He put the stars in their places. When land appeared, it wasn't simply to make us a comfortable dwelling place; it was a holy activity. Creation was not just a good-enough habitat for our survival; this place was consecrated.[8]

No other cosmogony handed a map of creation labeled "sacred" to humanity. Other cultures revered their cosmogonies as sacred stories telling them about their gods and their role in the world[9]—but none of those creation accounts stated that *the creation itself* was sacred.

Does this mean we need to take our shoes off when we step outside and wear prayer shawls as we farm? Of course not. But it may indicate that we have underestimated the miraculous gift our earth is. God starts with the perfect and ideal, and within that ideal, we will find a God we can trust with our whole selves.

How does a God who built a sacred cosmos also build eyelashes, tender tree roots, and sand dollars? Both the macro and the micro are delicately held in balance, their tender equilibrium keeping us humble and in awe. All these make me wonder at a God who delights in making beautiful and sacred things, and what's more, He wants *me* to know that He makes beautiful and sacred things. It is part of His character.

SMUDGED MAPS

When my kids were in elementary school, our kitchen table needed an upcycle. I purchased a large, artistic, and accurate map from Etsy and adhered it to the tabletop, adding many layers of shellac to protect it from the pounding I knew it would take. Unfortunately, when I put the shellac on, I somehow smeared Ireland, England, and Scotland into a multicolored smudge, forever making them one land mass in the Smith home.

My goal was to educate the kids about the world and remind them that our little house on our little street was part of a bigger globe. I imagined discussions about cultures and missionaries we loved, and wonder at the big wide world. Reality was not so sweet and tidy, though. Instead, my kids and their friends would declare countries for themselves, like a giant game of Monopoly. I sighed in resignation as I watched them turn into dictators eager to conquer entire hemispheres over dinner. Poor Djibouti was always claimed first, if only to say, "I own Ja-booty!" followed shortly by, "Don't forget about Ireland and England and Scotland, even though Mom tried to erase them!"

When the table smears or we find ourselves in foreign lands, sickness shadows our days, loved ones pass away, and the tsunamis of life hit, we can ground ourselves in the God of creation who reigns over it all. The map of sacred creation proclaims God's purposes, creating a contrast to our very real troubles and acknowledging that they were never part of the design. Just as God reigned over a sacred creation, God reigns over our smudged maps and broken environments.

Day seven is the only day of creation that doesn't end. The throne wasn't abandoned, and God's reign did not cease when humanity rejected the order He had established. The world was not thrown into chaos in Genesis 3. He remains enthroned—patient, holy, merciful, trustworthy, and powerful—drawing us back to His purposes with kindness (Rom. 2:4). When our hearts are aching, searching for a reprieve from our problems or a place to grieve our loss, day seven says: *rest here at the throne.*

Although day seven is still in effect, in a sense it's foggy. We travel through life carrying these two truths: God reigns, and life can be pretty hard. A foggy day seven means we live in both realities, walking around with smudged maps.

From Genesis, we learn about God's character—a character that has not changed even though the world you and I live in looks different than it did in the beginning. In the coming chapters, as we look at God's map (held right side up!) and His plan for His creation and us, we will see a remarkably trustworthy God.

This trustworthy God reigns over a creation where chaos has been controlled with ordinary words said by an all-powerful God. We will see how He calls us to interact with Him, remembering power is in God Himself, not in scripted prayers. He sits enthroned over an ecosystem perfectly put into place, organized simply, and pronounced good before humanity ever stepped foot in the garden. The plants He made were able to reproduce and provide for us, and He imbued us with purpose and dignity.

All of this sacred creation God declared good and blessed. All of this God did before He rested. This is the God you and I can trust with our chaos, prayers, provision, and purpose.

CHAPTER FOUR

SPEAKING TO CHAOS

GENESIS 1:1–2 {CHAOS}

THIS IS MY FATHER'S WORLD,
AND TO MY LISTENING EARS
ALL NATURE SINGS, AND ROUND ME RINGS
THE MUSIC OF THE SPHERES.

We had our kids very close together. Our first two, Stephen and Clara, were twenty-one months apart, and Abbie came along eleven months later. Three kids under three without a set of twins and with a hefty dose of naïveté. It's been fun, but the sheer exhaustion of it all erased entire years from my memory.

When the kids were in second, third, and fourth grade, our mornings were chaos no matter what I did. I tried setting out everything the night before, checklists, timers, threats, and straight-up begging. Part of the problem was that their bus didn't come until 8:45 in the morning, almost three hours into breakfast, play, and television. Getting into a school mindset in the morning was tricky when it was already snack time, and PBS Kids was calling.

After months of cajoling and trying everything I could think of (short of doing all the work for them), I told the kids they were on their own in the mornings from now on. They had the tools, they knew what to do, and it was time for natural consequences. They cheered, the poor dears. My husband, Brian, saluted me as he left for work the following day.

The next morning, I sat, drank my coffee, and watched the clock tick as the kids did their routine. They actually did pretty great and were almost ready by the time the bus was to arrive. But that darn PBS Kids pulled them in, and soon, the sound of the bus pulling up the street made them panic. I watched as they tore through the house, hollering and losing it. Stephen had a full, half-zipped backpack, arms loaded with paper, and a gallon-sized bag of goldfish, which he planned to use as trading currency at lunch. Clara started panting and made a valiant effort to tie her shoes quickly. Abbie (our most organized) realized they would miss the bus unless they dashed across the backyard to try and catch the bus at its *next* stop.

Doors slammed, and papers flew as the three raced across the backyard. A neighbor texted they had climbed onto the bus covered in sweat, beaming that they had made it. I turned off the TV and chuckled at the entire scenario. Our mornings were better after that. I chilled about their prep level, and everyone got on the same page about the importance of watching the time. And they never once missed the bus.

A constant state of chaos isn't fun, even if we know there is a plan B bus stop we can hit. Like me with my kids and our morning routine, we wonder two things: *What does order look like?* and *When disorder happens, how do we restore it back to order?* Creation stories are designed to answer these very questions in their ANE context.

NAMES AND THICKETS AND DESTINIES, OH MY!

All cosmogonies start with disorder or chaos. It doesn't have to be an adverse force; it can simply describe an unstructured place that needs order. Remember, to understand best *how* ancient Israelites received the very true Genesis account, we will read bits of other creation accounts told around campfires across the region.

Let's look at a cosmogony from Babylon we have called *Epic of Creation (Enuma Elish)* to show you what I mean. (If you're interested, you can check out the Cosmogony Quick Reference in the back for more info about this cosmogony.) It starts with disorder and chaos. The wording is different than we're used to, so I'll add a few comments to clarify what's happening.

Epic of Creation (Enuma Elish) text	Explanation
When on high no name was given to heaven, Nor below was the netherworld called by name,	When things don't have a name, they are without a role or function.
Primeval Apsu was their progenitor, And matrix-Tiamat was she who bore them all,	Apsu is the name for fresh water and a deity. A *progenitor* is a forefather. *Tiamat* is the watery deep and a deity.
They were mingling their waters together,	Salt water and fresh water are mixed.
No cand brake was intertwined nor thicket matted close.	This is describing the lack of dwellings.
When no gods at all had been brought forth, None called by names, none destinies ordained,[1]	When gods ordained destinies, they were establishing how the world would be ordered. That the destinies were not yet ordained meant a world without any order.

Initially, this certainly feels odd to read, but after looking through the explanations, give it another try. If you think about these words being uttered by your favorite storyteller (or someone like Gandalf from The Lord of the Rings or the grandfather from The Princess Bride) as you walk through the woods, they are inviting and intriguing.

Epic of Creation (Enuma Elish) starts by saying everything was nameless. The Babylonian people would have heard that as alarming disorder because a name indicates function (and namelessness equates to a lack of function).[2]

Brian and I experienced the same thing when our kids were toddlers, constantly asking with a pointed finger, "What's that? What's this? What does this do?" Their young minds were seeking the name and function of things because when the object did not belong to a category, it didn't mean anything to them. Until I answered and explained to my little ones what a coffeemaker was, they only knew it as a thing that beeps every morning and seemed to make Dad happy. Once I gave the object a name (coffeemaker) and function (makes the coffee that helps Daddy wake up), the thing was then able to fit organizationally into other categories (kitchen appliances).

Now imagine my most vocal toddler, Stephen, saying, "What's this?" and me repeatedly stating, "It doesn't have a name, and I don't know." The conversation would certainly escalate quickly! Now you have an idea of the disorder Enuma Elish is describing.

Besides being devoid of names and functions, things are also not where they should be. The text describes that fresh water and salt water are mixed, but the point is not that the salt water is now diluted. Rather, these two things are combined when they should be distinct and separate. And a few lines down, we learn there aren't buildings; the structure of homes and cities are not yet established. It's all a wilderness.

The description in *Enuma Elish* is like a child asking, "What's this?" and the answer is continuously, "I don't know." To the eye looking for something familiar, there is only water mixed wrong and no place for humanity to thrive. *Enuma Elish* has described an untenable way to live, and something needs to happen to bring order. Providing structure and order is the next step in the cosmogony genre, much like finding order was necessary for my kids to get themselves to the bus stop on time. Beyond storytelling, though, the *way* order happens provides a theological explanation of order.

ORDER UP

Enuma Elish is truly an epic story, with an involved plot describing how the world becomes ordered. We won't go into the details, but as a summary, the gods Apsu and Tiamat make other gods (more on this later) until a genealogy appears.[3] Conflict erupts when the deities grow up, and a new form of chaos emerges.[4] The rest of the story describes how the world becomes settled and peaceful, with gods using a lot of diplomacy[5] (with both good[6] and bad advisors[7]), magic words,[8] wisdom,[9] and violence.[10] At the end of the tale, the god Marduk triumphs, takes the throne, and is praised by all the other gods.

Recall that these creation accounts were meant to instruct people on how to live and help them relate to their gods and their world. Keeping that in mind, *Enuma Elish* made sense to the Babylonian people as a theological document. It answered our two questions: *What does order look like?* and *When disorder happens, how do I restore it?*

To the Babylonians, order looked like a solar system that was in place, a sun that rose every day, and predictable seasons. Order was experienced in a physical world with rhythms that made producing crops and working livestock viable. A city with a functioning temple was always a part of an ordered world. Falling in line with the world's created stability was the way to thrive. If people minded their own business and sought their own welfare, then life was pleasant, good, and praiseworthy.

If a Babylonian child asked his dad how he knew when to plant or how they could navigate directions with the stars, his father may have put his arm around his son and started his answer with a story, "When on high no name was given to heaven, / Nor below was the netherworld called by name . . ."[11] *Enuma Elish* answered the boy's questions by creatively telling him about the order put in place by the gods.

The methods of diplomacy, magic words, wisdom, and violence to achieve this order would be comforting. To a Babylonian, the gods were powerful and able to handle cosmic chaos using force if necessary; they had magic words (or secret knowledge) and wisdom available to them.

Magic or secret knowledge was not considered the opposite of religion in the ANE; it was considered a part of religion. Priests were involved in temple rituals and incantations; they worked as scribes and pharmacists.[12] Where we may put these jobs into separate categories, these were all intricately intertwined to the ANE person.

See how a Babylonian poem expresses a man's distress and the places he sought relief when he became quite ill:

My omens were confused, they were contradictory every day,
The prognostication of diviner and dream interpreter could
not explain what I was undergoing.

What was said in the street portended ill for me, When I lay down at night, my dream was terrifying.[13]

For the Babylonians, order was restored by seeking the help of their gods, using the professional guidance of priests, diviners, and interpreters. Omens were typically solicited when a person wanted advice or direction from a deity. In many cases, a diviner (or other professional) would kill an animal and then examine the intestines for specific signs. Sometimes, an omen was in the form of an astronomical event or a birth defect. If disruption struck (like a disease, war, or natural disaster), the Babylonians would seek out priests who could go to a deity for help. These trained priests could use their resources and books to read omens, interpret dreams, and read the stars.

Between religious activity, advisors, warfare, diplomacy, and wisdom, their cosmogony certainly answered questions about what order looked like and how to get it back. Understood this way, my version of stopping the chaos in my house and getting my kids to the bus on time was like the methods used in Babylonian accounts. I didn't use omens or anything, but I was focused on alleviating my frustrations through diplomacy and wisdom. I'm *not* saying that the theology of Babylonians is *my* theology, only that their methods for bringing about order in their lives, as taken from the examples of their deities, were practical. They were compelling enough solutions that humanity has been using those same methods for thousands of years.

GREAT POTENTIAL

Egyptian cosmogonies also start with chaos. Theirs begin with water and darkness, a chaotic primal condition.[14] In their creative process, Egyptian stories lean more toward peaceful ways to bring order than the Babylonian accounts.[15] There is no fighting, politicking, or disruption. The beginning is simply a pre-creation "single source"[16] that needs to be arranged.

One way the Egyptian gods ordered the world was through divine words. These words were similar to the magic words of *Enuma Elish* in that they were able to create.[17] Unique to Egyptian views, however, was that the elements that needed ordering had potential in themselves. The god spoke to water, and the water spoke back before it was formed correctly.[18] Look below for a few verses in Egyptian texts to see how the god Atum ordered the world:

Perception is his heart, Annunciation his lips.
His energy (ka) is that which exists through his tongue.[19]

He began speaking in the midst of silence,
opening every eye and causing them to look.
He began crying out while the world was in stillness,
his yell in circulation while he had no second,
that he might give birth to what is and cause them to live,
and cause every person to know the way to walk.[20]

The god Atum saw in his heart that something needed to be done (perception) and then followed through with his speech (annunciation).[21] In the Egyptian worldview, the pre-created existing state was full of potential, waiting for a god to bring order by speaking.

When we lived in the Midwest, our homes were notoriously dry in the winter because running the furnace sucks out all the moisture in the air. This dry atmosphere made touching a shopping cart in Target or Walmart an exercise in bravery. More often than not, I grimaced as I put my finger on the cart handle, knowing I could give myself a solid static shock by touching it. In our home, Brian learned to touch my hand before giving me a peck on the cheek. A jolt on the hand is way better than one on the face. I love the guy, but I didn't care for shocking kisses. The electric potential that was in my home is a little like the potential described in Egyptian cosmogonies. It is intrinsic in the environment, just waiting for the deity to access it.

The simpler Egyptian creation accounts answer our two questions: *What does order look like?* and *When disorder happens, how do I restore it?* Like the Babylonians, order is seen in the rhythms and predictability of the seasons. Egyptians believed Atum (or Ptah[22]) put the world in order, whereas Babylonians believed Marduk did. Both thought that to thrive was to live according to the seasons and anticipate their certainty by planting and harvesting at the appropriate time. They let the stars guide them as they traveled, worked, and played.

Individually, when an Egyptian man or woman had disorder in their own lives, they would petition various deities using similar methods as the Babylonians. They found a priest who used rituals designed to bring a benefit and provide peace.[23] These priests had access to the sacred writings (literally "words of the gods") only kept in temples. These rituals were required to be kept secret and written in a language only the priests could read because the knowledge of such things was power.[24] Ultimately, these rituals were performed for the betterment of the people of Egypt; they were designed to bring order back into the chaos that invaded lives.[25]

GENESIS

Now that we've listened in on some of the other stories around the campfire, it's time to listen to Genesis with new ears. Maybe even say these words aloud as if you are speaking them to a child who has never heard them before:

In the beginning God created the heavens and the earth. The earth was formless and void, and darkness was over the surface of the deep, and the Spirit of God was moving over the surface of the waters. (Gen. 1:1–2)

Maybe you've never read "formless," "void," "darkness," and "surface of the deep" as anything other than an exciting way to start a story. Still, those terms and that sentence were communicating to the varied ANE cultures that there was chaos in the beginning. A chaos that required God to create and bring order to it.

With this, Genesis sticks to the cosmogony genre styling. The beginning of the story sets the tone, like how a fairy tale cues the readers with, "Once upon a time." By participating in the genre as the audience knew it, it was clear what the story was doing. This was a theological story telling them how the world came into being. It's like saying to the audience, "Heads up! Creation story starting!"

As we've been learning, *how* God brings order teaches us about Him and how we interact in this world. So, what does He do?

	Genesis	Cosmogony Category[26]
1:3	*Then God said, "Let there be light"; and there was light*	*Creation by word*
1:4	*God saw that the light was good; and God separated the light from the darkness.*	*Separation: organization*
1:5	*God called the light day, and the darkness He called night. And there was evening and there was morning, one day.*	*Naming: organization*

A glance at the chart pairing up Genesis verses with the cosmogony categories reveals a lot of similarities between Genesis and other accounts. God uses words to create, He separates, and He names. Around the ANE campfire, there would have been nodding and listening, with a few head tilts. The main job of the deity in cosmogony accounts is to bring order to a chaotic beginning, and Genesis checks all the right genre boxes.

In many ways, the lesson to ancient Israel about the nature of order in the universe was the same as the lessons in other cosmogonies. The seasons were stable, and planting and harvesting would be predictable. The stars would give directions; the moon would pull the tides. Day and night would happen with certainty. In cosmogonies, all gods were gods of order. Other ANE cultures believed their gods put the order into place; Genesis says it was only one—Yahweh.

This draw to orderliness is inherent in our culture too. We are all glad that the sun will rise in the morning and crops will be harvested yearly. We don't freak out when the leaves turn red and orange and fall off trees because we know they will come back in the spring with brilliant green. An environment with rhythms we can connect to helps everyone in that environment, not just those who believe in the God of Genesis.

I love how God lets seasons and good things testify about His character to everyone, not just His people (Acts 14:16–17). Like a special flower delivery in our yard and our neighbor's yard, God delights to bless. He is consistent and trustworthy, regardless of our allegiance.

SAY WHAT?

Our love of order in nature may be the same across time and culture; however, there is one very unusual feature in the Genesis ordering: God spoke the words.

No other creation story tells us the words their gods used as they created. Babylonian stories mention that gods used words to call things to order, and in Egyptian cosmogonies, the god speaks and calls a force into life. If you wanted to know what those words were, though, you'd be plumb out of luck. Those words are powerful and not to be shared; they belong to the god and will stay with him.

But in Genesis, God reveals the words like it's no big deal. It's almost like He's daring you to try and say them. Would a bright light appear if a child whispered, "Let there be light," as if they were magic words? Nope. God is not afraid to let people know the words because the terms do not have intrinsic power. God's ability to create, order, and give purpose is inherent.

With this small move, God undercuts the idea that there is secret knowledge or words with power. By saying, "Let there be light," He is telling us there isn't a mysterious phrase only available to the deity that makes light. Rather, *He* is the source of that ability to create.

In the ancient world, the availability of secret knowledge provided an access point between the physical and spiritual worlds. God's push against special or concealed words may have felt defeating or frustrating because it eliminated a significant source of help for the wide-ranging ancient cultures. When facing illness, drought, famine, and war, it would have been natural to seek a direct line of communication with anyone who might be in charge. Like us, when we were overwhelmed during our Year of Cancer, they just wanted relief and for the pain to stop. They wanted the world back in order and a way to ask their god how to get it.

God welcomes our communication and interactions with Him, but in Genesis 1, He took omens and spells off the table. With two little Hebrew words translated as "let there be light," God redrew the landscape of religion. God shook His head "no" to a significant piece of the ANE religious worlds, including a prominent aspect of ANE priestly roles.

SET UP TO RUN WELL

When God undermined the idea of secret knowledge and magic words, He didn't fill in the blanks for what to do in Genesis 1. I imagine the campfire crowd was a little put out that there wasn't a solution for correctly interacting with God when they needed help with real problems.

Remember our two primary questions cosmogonies answer? *What does order look like?* and *When disorder happens, how do I restore it?* Genesis 1 appears to answer only one of them. It tells us what order looks like. The ANE listeners knew what *not* to do (omens and secret knowledge), but they didn't know what *to* do. Genesis 1 doesn't explain how to put life back together when the bottom falls out from under us, which might seem a little unsettling, but there's a reason for that.

Genesis 1 doesn't address how to restore order because it describes how the world is *supposed* to be. It describes God putting things into their designed place and in their proper sequence. It explains how things ought to be.

Enuma Elish, Egyptian cosmogonies, and ANE creation accounts described how the world *is*. They gave evidence for chaotic events (the gods were fighting) or droughts (the gods were upset) and then provided theology for addressing those problems. And their answers made sense! They include politicking, violence, and secret access to the gods when things go wrong. According to these cosmogonies, the world we live in, with all its turbulence, *is the design.*

Not so with Genesis. Like the maps analogy from chapter 3, God's sacred map of creation doesn't have plan B bus stops for when a crisis hits because His design doesn't include reoccurring disasters. From the beginning, God designed an order that was good and complete—but His is not a bland and uptight order. He designed the earth to be lovely and beautiful and generous and predictable. He planned for flourishing.

Goodness, I love this about God. It means that when I pray for my family, whatever He determines for them will come from the same hand that designed sunsets. If I feel helpless about my circumstances, my heart can rest as I bring my concerns to the God who invented flourishing. God has shown me who He is when He ordered the universe, and I don't have to search out secrets or locate a professional for access. He Himself is the source and is evident to anyone.

PLEASE AND THANK YOU

To answer our question—*When disorder happens, how do I restore it?*—we have to keep turning the pages in our Bibles past Genesis 1. Regarding the ANE culturally accepted methods of diviners and omens (direction from the gods), God is consistent with His creation principle. He continued to prohibit mediums or spiritualists with secret knowledge (Lev. 19:31; 20:6; Deut. 18:10–14). Additionally, God required the entrails and liver (Lev. 1:9, 13; 3:6–17) to be burned in sacrifices, as most cultures would look at livers and intestines for omens. Secret knowledge was not supposed to be a thing for Israel. Pause momentarily and think about God forbidding a significant industry that aided people. It would have been quite disorienting.

Israel did not heed God's instructions. King Saul consulted a medium when faced with a frightening battle (1 Sam. 28:5–25). King Manassah "practiced witchcraft, used divination, practiced sorcery and dealt with mediums and spiritists" (2 Chron. 33:6). And the prophet Isaiah had a stern warning for the people of Judah:

> When they say to you, "Consult the mediums and the spiritists who whisper and mutter," should not a people consult their God? Should they consult the dead on behalf of the living? To the law and to the testimony! If they do not speak according to this word, it is because they have no dawn. (Isa. 8:19–20)

So, what does God ask us to do when the bottom falls out from under us? The example of a man named Job, who was praised for his righteousness (Job 1:1) and encountered personal and economic devastation, answers that very question. He did not seek out a diviner or omen, and he didn't ask a priest to read the stars or interpret his dreams using their books with divine explanations. Instead, he talked to his wife and his friends. And importantly, he talked directly to God. That's it. God was calling Israel (and us) to interact with Him directly.

In the New Testament, when the disciples asked Jesus how they should pray, He gave them the Lord's Prayer (Matt. 6:9–13; Luke 11:1–4). It wasn't a magic prayer with words that needed to be recited to access God. According to Oxford theologian Dr. N. T. Wright, it "serves as a lens through which to see Jesus himself, and to discover something of what he was about."[27]

After Luke's version of the Lord's Prayer, Jesus gave metaphors and examples of how prayer works. In one example, shameless audacity led to the effectiveness of the petitioner (Luke 11:5–8). In another, Jesus reminded the disciples that God loves to give good gifts to His children (Luke 11:11–13). As Pete Greig says in his book on prayer, "Keep it real, keep it simple, keep it up."[28] I think Job would have agreed.

The prayers in the Bible or even prayers recited during a liturgical church service offer examples and insights into how we relate with God; they are not meant to be used as formulas for success. Similarly, the "sinner's prayer" is helpful for those who have never prayed before, but the words and their specific order do not save anyone. God cares about belief and a contrite heart (Rom. 10:9; Ps. 51:15–17).

When I was growing up, if my parents asked for "the magic words," I would quickly say, "Please" or "Thank you," knowing it would precipitate whatever I was asking for. Of course, the words weren't magic, and my parents certainly weren't teaching me sorcery. They were training me to be polite and automatically say these words. In a way, magic was shorthand for effective. They could have just as easily said, "Say the effective words!" My parents knew the word "please" would soften my request, help me remember my position in the relationship as a recipient, and generally help things go well for me in life. Adding a "thank you" never hurt anyone, either. I've certainly taught my kids the same way! Out of curiosity, the other day I asked Abbie (now eighteen) what the magic words were, and without hesitation, she said, "Please and thank you."

We like effective and efficient because they feel powerful. Glance at an influential pastor's page after a retreat, conference, or seminar, and you'll likely find the word *powerful* streaked across it. We are drawn to places where we can feel heard or our prayers are impactful. And that's when times are going smoothly enough! We hit the praying hand emojis hard when a crisis, small or large, hits. If the paycheck isn't enough to cover the bills and the car breaks, or when a sickness strikes a loved one, we don't just want to pray and hope; we want prayers that will have guaranteed results.

And to be honest, that sounds pretty good to me.

It would be lovely if reciting the prayer of Jabez (1 Chron. 4:10) released God's miraculous power in my life. I'd love to know that if I said "in Jesus' name" at the end of every prayer, my requests would be granted (a common misunderstanding of John 16:23–24). I sometimes wish that everyone who recited the "sinner's prayer," whether they believed it or not, was automatically aligned with Jesus. And I sure as anything would love it if whatever I named and claimed became mine. But I believe God is quietly shaking His head at me in Genesis 1 and the rest of His Word. That's not how He works. God Himself is the source of power, not special words said in a certain order.

God knows we live with smudged maps, forced to take detours around both small irritants and life-altering traumas. He wants us to keep coming to Him when our life feels disordered because *in Himself* is the power and the compassion. Our very good Father wants us to come as we are with our needs, and He wants us to reject the secret formulas and magic words. He does not respond to manipulation or keep Himself hidden. God's desire for a relationship with us is as startling to us as it was to the ANE listeners—we have direct access to the One who put the stars in place and created light with two little Hebrew words.

Communicating with God about our smudged maps is as simple and wonderful (and maybe even intimidating) as honestly approaching God and talking to Him. What an absolute marvel.

> Give ear, O LORD, to my prayer;
> And give heed to the voice of my supplications!
> In the day of my trouble I shall call upon You,
> For You will answer me.
> There is no one like You among the gods, O Lord,
> Nor are there any works like Yours. (Ps. 86:6–8)

CHAPTER FIVE

INCONCEIVABLE!

GENESIS 1:3–13 {DAYS ONE, TWO, AND THREE}

BY THE WORD OF THE LORD THE HEAVENS WERE MADE,
AND BY THE BREATH OF HIS MOUTH ALL THEIR HOST.
HE GATHERS THE WATERS OF THE SEA TOGETHER AS A HEAP;
HE LAYS UP THE DEEPS IN STOREHOUSES.
LET ALL THE EARTH FEAR THE LORD;
LET ALL THE INHABITANTS OF THE WORLD STAND IN AWE OF HIM.
FOR HE SPOKE, AND IT WAS DONE;
HE COMMANDED, AND IT STOOD FAST. (PS. 33:6–9)

My daughter Abbie loves order. As a preschooler, her favorite toy was a yellow legal pad, and she walked around all day asking me and our dog questions, making check marks after we responded. I purchased her stocking stuffers from Office Max, filling her stocking with new staplers, three-hole punchers, and tape. The girl liked to have everything in its right place. So, it was unsurprising when she asked if she could have a budget to reorganize her closet when she got to high school.

The first job was to empty her closet and take measurements. After that, Abbie found dimensions for a set of drawers and marked areas with painter's tape to ensure they would fit along with curtain rods and shelves. Finally, she put away her books and clothes. Keep in mind that this was not a large closet. In fact, it was the smallest in our home. But because of her strategic planning and use of space, it became our most efficient area.

As we exit the initial chaos found at the beginning of creation, let me invite you to picture it as an empty closet. How would you first start to organize it? (If you're like me and less organized than Abbie, don't get overwhelmed. It's just an example.) You'd probably start by installing a rod for hangers, shelves for folded clothing, and maybe a place to drop off laundry. The first step is to allocate areas for things, provide appropriate places, and fill those spaces later. Creation accounts also begin with a similar order.

Two primary structures that cosmologies needed to find a spot for were water (rivers and oceans as well as rain) and land. These things needed to be in their place before any other parts of the earth could be accounted for, such as fish, birds, or humanity. Land and water, however, were understood much differently than they are today. In their conception of the earth, ANE cultures experienced the world as flat, with the primary analogy of a solid dome to explain the reality of the atmosphere that held back the water above. Let's see how Egypt, Babylon, and Genesis presented their organization.

EGYPT

Egypt's stories told of a god of the atmosphere (named Shu) who held up the sky (called Nut) while standing on the earth (personified as Geb). In one text, it reads:

I am weary at the Uplifting of Shu,
since I lifted my daughter Nut atop me
that I might give her to my father Atum in his utmost extent.
I have put Geb under my feet:
this god is tying together the land for my father Atum.[1]

Sky god–Nut

Air god–
Shu

Earth god–
Geb

"Greenfield Papyrus" on display at the British Museum.
"An image of the sky goddess Nut arched over the earth god
Geb, with the god Shu supporting the sky between them."[2]
Public domain.

We can see the dome shape made by the sky as Shu stood over the earth. Picturing the world in this shape with a place for the waters and the land was standard thinking.

BABYLON

In Babylon, they experienced the world as flat, with the sky above in a dome shape (just as we do when we step outside our front door). In *Enuma Elish*, the firmament and land formed after a great battle between Marduk and Tiamat. Marduk won and then split the carcass of Tiamat to create the sky above and the land/sea below. According to this myth, the earth, ocean, and sky are the disposed carcass of a great and powerful god.

Tiamat and Marduk, sage of the gods, drew close for battle,
They locked in single combat, joining for the fray.
. . .
The Lord [Marduk] trampled upon the frame of Tiamat,
With his merciless mace he crushed her skull.
He cut open the arteries of her blood,
. . .
He split her in two, like a fish for drying,
Half of her he set up and made as a cover, heaven.
He stretched out the hide and assigned watchmen,
And ordered them not to let her waters escape.
He crossed heaven and inspected (its) firmament.[3]

GENESIS

The ancient Israelites also thought of the world using the primary analogy of a solid dome.[4] God did not challenge this thinking by completely reorienting their understanding of the universe. Instead, Genesis slips into the logical structure of cosmogonies. God was addressing more significant theological issues within the culture, not scientific misunderstandings (see the Twenty-First-Century Questions on p. 173).

To divide the waters above and waters below, God placed an expanse:

Then God said, "Let there be an expanse in the midst of the waters, and let it separate the waters from the waters." God made the expanse, and separated the waters which were below the expanse from the waters which were above the expanse; and it was so. (Gen. 1:6–7)

The separation of the sea and sky, translated as *expanse* in the NASB, is the Hebrew word *rāqîaʿ* (pronounced rah-KEE-ah). This is a tricky word to translate, and you'll find different versions using different words (NIV: *vault*; NET, NASB: *expanse*; NLT: *space*; NRSV: *dome*). A Hebrew lexicon explains that *rāqîaʿ* "was understood as the gigantic heavenly dome which was the source of the light that brooded over the heavenly ocean and of which the dome arched above the earthly globe."[5]

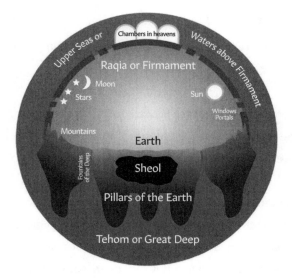

Hebrew Understanding of the Cosmos, creative common use, Tom Lemmens

As we look at the first three days, we can note the initial organizational structure being set up. Next, we watch the hanging rod installation, and only later will we see the hangers with shirts and pants fill up the space allotted for them. As Dr. Sandra Richter, professor of Old Testament at Westmont College, says in her book *The Epic of Eden*, the created order is "first according to their habitats and then according to their inhabitants."[6]

The creation account in Genesis unfolds logically, which is typical of ANE cosmogonies. In the first days, God creates distinct spaces and areas; the following three days, He fills those spaces.[7] On day seven, God rests, declaring His creative process complete and ready to run.

Habitat	Inhabitants
Day 1 (time): Day and Night	**Day 4**: Sun, Moon, and Stars
Day 2 (climate): Sea and Sky	**Day 5**: Fish and Birds
Day 3 (agriculture): Land and Vegetation	**Day 6**: Animals and Humanity
Day 7: Rest	

Days one to three provide an initial structure and offer us two of the most essential elements for our survival—climate and agriculture.[8] We depend entirely on God for these parts of our existence. The weather, time, and sustenance must all be held in a delicate balance for us to survive. The ancients knew this as well as we do, and maybe even more so, as they were an agrarian society.

All cosmogonies recognize this need for structure and elements of survival. However, God does something different in Genesis because these components are not delegated to other gods. The atmosphere is not a living god or a defeated god. They are elements under His control, designed by Him. The simplicity of Genesis, God simply moving the waters into their places and providing habitats for later inhabitants, starkly contrasts the complexity of the pantheistic universes put into place by other cosmogonies.

The order of Genesis days one and two fit into the typical cosmogony genre, but day three starts to veer in a different direction.

Structurally, it provided a habitat, but where it made a switch was when it took pains to stress that the vegetation is reliably self-perpetuating. Other cosmogonies are aware of the nature of the land and vegetation, but Genesis lays one specific difference on thick.

> Then God said, "Let the waters below the heavens be gathered into one place, and let the dry land appear"; and it was so. God called the dry land earth, and the gathering of the waters He called seas; and God saw that it was good. Then God said, "Let the earth sprout vegetation, plants yielding seed, and fruit trees on the earth bearing fruit after their kind with seed in them"; and it was so. The earth brought forth vegetation, plants yielding seed after their kind, and trees bearing fruit with seed in them, after their kind; and God saw that it was good. There was evening and there was morning, a third day. (Gen. 1:9–13)

After the seas were gathered together, land appeared, both were named, and God saw it was good. Then, verses 11 and 12 take pains to describe the self-perpetuating cycle placed within vegetation, and God was pleased. To ANE cultures, the goodness of vegetation described in Genesis was unique and undoubtedly lovely. Other cosmogonies do not have this sense of divine pleasure at creation for creation itself; they are often tied to the gods' service or ease.

Genesis jumps at the chance to repeatedly remind us that what God created, He also declared good. Beyond the inherent beauty in appearance and design, the goodness of creation reflects a good Creator.

From day three, fruitfulness was the responsibility of God.

Adam and Eve weren't placed on barren land with soil and a handful of seeds and told to figure it out. The earth was already functional and ready to go. On God's Word, the earth sprouted vegetation, trees grew, and fruit reproduced. Before humanity or animals were added to the mix, each habitat flourished and was set up to run and to run well. They didn't need to hunt down a hoe, shovel, or dig an irrigation canal for their first meal. God provided everything necessary. When God rested and established His reign over a good world, creation was not set up as an acrimonious relationship between man and nature.[9] It was designed to work harmoniously, a habitat where flourishing was ordained. Humankind would work in tandem with it.

Picturing their reality stretches the mind. Imagine yourself tending to God's good soil, where everything flourishes as it should. In the beginning, there was enough food for every day. It all worked when working in tandem with God's good soil. Vegetation was good whether it was used as sustenance or not.

Now, use your imagination to connect that predictable thriving to our work and efforts. It's almost impossible for me to picture sitting down and writing without struggle, much less flourishing in every area God has asked me to tend to. What a delight it would be to cultivate with assurance and ease. I imagine you feel the same way.

When my organized daughter put together her spectacularly designed closet, it wasn't complete until it was filled with its contents. But you can be sure we stepped back and admired the design before filling the drawers. We have that same opportunity here to look at the first three days and note that the habitats God created were good even before they were inhabited because God is good. It was designed to run well and to be a well-ordered environment for its occupants. This is the sense of good in the creation account. Everything God created He declared good because it acted within its purpose and provided benefits. The seas are good because they are in their correct spot, and a good God made them. The apple trees are good because they bear apples, and the apples are good because they have seeds within them, and most importantly, the whole tree and the apples are good because God is good. It's pleasing and suitable for the land to produce reproducing fruits, for light to separate from darkness, and to provide a place for the sun. From top to bottom, His creation shouts that there is a good Creator!

DEEP WATER

But if you're like me, sometimes it's just hard to accept that God is good.

As a college sophomore, I took a college-sponsored mission trip to Jamaica. About ten brawny baseball players and a few of us girls traveled for a January break from the cold Indiana winds. After completing our work at a half-dead church, we were gifted a two-night stay at an all-inclusive resort.

A waterfall climb popular with tourists was on our agenda. We rode the resort van over, read the warning signs, and started to climb barefoot. The families, led by guides, walked safely, hand in hand, up the side of the falls. We chose to walk without a guide right up the middle, purposefully ignoring the warning signs. Together, we climbed the enormous rocks as the warm water rushed past our strong calves, thighs, and sometimes even our hips. I was young and light and invincible.

As we approached one particularly high waterfall, the guides motioned to us and called, "Come to the side!" We smiled and waved that we knew what we were doing. As we climbed, bare feet placed on rocks, the tallest and strongest in our group went first along the flowing path. From behind, I estimated the coming waterfall to be five and a half feet. About my height, maybe a bit shorter. Easy.

The strongest guy reached down and helped a friend ahead of me who was struggling. I reevaluated: maybe it was six feet.

A few more triumphed and climbed breathless and exhilarated.

The last in the line, I confidently made my way to the bottom of the rocks and began to ascend. I realized too late that it was at least seven feet. As I made my way, it was suddenly clear that I could not find a rock to grab and propel myself upward. Turning my head up, looking for a rock to grasp, I instantly felt the torrent hit me full in the face. I would have to keep my head down.

Had the rest moved on, ready for the next challenge? I was blind in a waterfall without a way up or down.

Suddenly, a memory from childhood that I had pushed down bubbled up. I was shoved underwater by a playmate, my head submerged with fingers entwined in my hair. My strong lungs allowed me to wait passively, determined to prove my strength and reserve. Keeping calm, I felt powerful—until my lungs started to fail. I suddenly was frantic and terrified, and desperation overtook me, and I clawed at his arm. He let go, and I sputtered up, crying furious tears.

In Jamaica, I felt my lungs fail again, and the corresponding urgency and panic rise. My only option was to hold my arm up high and hope.

I raised my hand, waving my fingers, and reached into the air and ricocheting water drops. I made silent and wordless pleas only I could hear. I recalled the guides and their concerned looks. This was what they knew, what they tried to prevent.

A strong hand clasped mine, sure and firm. Then another hand grabbed my other forearm, and I released entirely from the rocks, wrapping my hand around my rescuer's forearm. My feet found footing, and I climbed as they lifted while lying on their bellies at the top of the waterfall. Standing, they pulled me up. All the while, my head was down, water flowing down my back.

At the top, I sheepishly looked at the smiling baseball players. They were still exhilarated at the adventure. They had not perceived the danger I felt.

I was terrified.

Since then, I've enjoyed beaches, but the thought of deep water still makes me a touch panicky. I'll listen to the waves crash and marvel at the sea's power and the moon's pull. But the shore feels safe, and I'm content to keep it in sight.

I know God directs the sea, but it's hard to imagine sometimes when I've never seen God miraculously control the waves. Perhaps this is why the disciples shook in their boots when Jesus walked across a wind-tossed sea (see Matt. 14:22–33). If they were harboring any doubt about Jesus' identity, in walking across the Sea of Galilee, He was declaring loud and clear that He was with God in the beginning (see John 1:1–5).[10]

The book of Matthew recounts that Jesus sent His disciples ahead of Him on a boat while He stayed at a mountainside to pray. The wind blew strong across the sea, creating waves that tossed their boat. Presumably unaffected by the weather or the waves, Jesus walked to their boat. When they saw Him, they thought perhaps He was a ghost, but Jesus told them, "Take courage, it is I; do not be afraid" (Matt. 14:27). The translation of "it is I" could also be translated "I Am," the words God used to identify Himself to Moses.

The disciple Peter, incredibly, asks for proof. "Lord, if it is You, command me to come to You on the water" (Matt. 14:28). With bold faith, Peter steps onto the water and walks to Jesus.

One of the things that strikes me about this story is that when Peter steps onto the water, the wind is still blowing hard, and the boat is still being tossed. I imagine the scene was hectic as the other disciples were laboring to keep the boat afloat, alarmed by Jesus walking across the sea and maybe watching with bated breath as Peter boldly put a foot over the side.

It must have been something to watch the scene play out. God in human form stood calmly on the seas with waves rising, Peter climbing out and somehow also able to stand and walk on liquid as the wind howled around him. And Peter did pretty great—he certainly showed more courage than the other disciples!—until he was reminded of the wind's terrible power and began to sink. And sinking, he cried out, "Lord, save me!" Immediately, Jesus stretched out His hand, took hold of Peter, and said, "You of little faith, why did you doubt?" (Matt. 14:30b–31).

Jesus caught Peter and saved him, and together, they walked to the boat. Did you notice, though, that the wind was still blowing and the waves were still crashing even after Jesus helped Peter? The weather was volatile throughout the entire passage.

Until Jesus got to the boat, and then the wind stopped.[11] "And those who were in the boat worshiped Him, saying, 'You are certainly God's Son!'" (Matt. 14:33).

It seems like the disciples finally understood to their core that Jesus was God. I wonder, though, if their reaction was more instinctive than cerebral. Perhaps they couldn't help but fall down and worship after the experience. The wind had stopped, and an awe fell over them all. There was no other possible response than to revere their Creator God in the flesh.

The storm kept raging when Peter had faith, when he remembered the wind, *and* after Jesus saved him. Peter's faith did not affect the storm.

"WHEN SORROWS LIKE SEA BILLOWS ROLL"[12]

Having felt the physical realities of deep water, I can testify that the storms of life can feel just as overwhelming to your soul.[13] When Clara's cancer was revealed to us, I absolutely felt despair that took my very breath. But after she was declared NED (No Evidence of Disease) and our lives returned to a new post-cancer normal, I hit another round of deep water. This one was just between me and God.

During Clara's treatment, I was deeply sad, but I didn't have the emotional bandwidth to do much but cry and push it down. I held on to my deep questions and pain until the year after Clara finished with chemo, and then I experienced a grief-induced faith upheaval. It would have been rage-induced, but honestly, I was too tired to be angry. In the reprieve of the crisis and one-foot-in-front-of-the-other survival, the house would quiet after the kids hopped on the bus, and I sat in my red rocking chair. Mostly, I grieved and confessed to feeling betrayed. How could this have happened?

As someone who lives in her head a bit, I struggled to handle the apparent paradox of our reality over the previous year. It was true that Clara had battled cancer (and all that encompasses). It was also true that God was good. Try as I might, I could not hold those both at the same time without feeling intellectually dishonest or foolish. It felt like someone was playing two piano keys next to each other over and over, making a dissonant sound in my soul.

Growing up in church, I knew the right verses and phrases, but they felt shallow and trite when I looked at my bald little girl or her defeated siblings. And so, for months, I sat and rocked. I prayed without words, sometimes holding both truths of my reality up in the air, asking God to grant me peace. For hours and hours, I made myself more and more vulnerable before God, sometimes lying on the floor sobbing.

This was my storm on the Sea of Galilee. The waves were real, *and* Jesus was real.

LIVING WITH THE DISSONANCE

Somehow, instead of forcing me to choose one truth or the other, God showed me that part of living here on earth is to live with dissonance. Both things were true, holding weight. God is good. *And* my sweet six-year-old had battled cancer.

For some reason, I thought God would insist that I ignore or, at the very least, minimize the pain our family endured. I thought my questions meant my faith wasn't very good, and I was sinking. Now I realize, though, that like Peter, by holding both my hands up, I was walking toward God as the waves crashed by letting Him in on my faith struggle. I was holding up the scalding memories and the disappointments, finally ready to encounter my deep grief. He could handle it, and I trusted Him.

We won't sink when we look to Jesus as the winds howl. But Peter taught us that we *can* sink when the winds become our solitary focus. When our problem is the only truth we hold up, we will come to the end of ourselves very quickly. Gracious Jesus is still there, though, reaching out a hand when we call out for help.

My encounter with creation has been like that of the disciples after Jesus returned to the boat. The winds quieted, revealing a powerful and *good* God—and, in awe, I worshiped. His character, as revealed in creation, has grown my trust, somehow making the dissonance bearable. I can look up and say, "Hear that, God? I can't wait for that situation to be redeemed." And I think He nods in agreement.

But it's hard sometimes, right? There are days when everything is a struggle, and each step feels like quicksand. We can't get ahead on our finances, the kids are fighting nonstop, and then the dishwasher breaks. It's enough to make us throw our hands up and pull out a pint of ice cream.

Creation teaches us that our frustration is appropriate; we are irritated because what we experience is disordered. The slog we face and the environments we fight are symptoms that show life is not ordered as intended. When we shout with exasperation, "It's not supposed to be this way!" God nods. He agrees; it's not supposed to be this way.

This is *not* a fatalistic view, though—it is a hopeful perspective. We don't hang our heads in defeat, shrugging because "it is what it is." No! We say, "Thank God it's not supposed to be this way." The disorders of broken relationships, the unhoused, food insecurity, and epidemics are not what God intended for us, and thankfully, we serve a God who redeems and restores. In Romans 8:20–25, nature gives us our cue:

> For the creation was subjected to futility, not willingly, but because of Him who subjected it, in hope that the creation itself also will be set free from its slavery to corruption into the freedom of the glory of the children of God. For we know that the whole creation groans and suffers the pains of childbirth together until now. And not only this, but also

we ourselves, having the first fruits of the Spirit, even we ourselves groan within ourselves, waiting eagerly for our adoption as sons, the redemption of our body. For in hope we have been saved, but hope that is seen is not hope; for who hopes for what he already sees? But if we hope for what we do not see, with perseverance we wait eagerly for it.

Creation feels the futility right along with us and longs for the restoration of life back on days one through seven. The groaning and suffering are the result of our choice in Genesis 3 (more on this later), but creation doesn't groan in despair; it groans in hope. Did you catch *why* creation's subjection was *in hope*? "Because of Him who subjected it." God, whose character does not change (Mal. 3:6; James 1:17), is still in charge. We can trust Him, His definition of order, and His purposes. As we all sit *in* creation and *with* creation, we hope, relying on the character of God, who works things for good and redeems everything He made. Creation will be restored, as will we. This present reality is not the end of the story because God is on the throne, and His character gives us hope.

Let Genesis 1 frame our "supposed to be" so that we can orient ourselves when frustrations are overwhelming. Creation teaches us what order is supposed to look like and about the God who put it all into place. When we are well acquainted with God and how He designed the world to work, we will start to get good at spotting disorder. The good, intended order that God put into place allows us to sense when things are out of order.

I still have deep griefs, some about our family's cancer journey, some about other events. All of which are too tender to share here and will probably never be public. I imagine you have some of those too. Places that are healed enough to function but will remain tender until God can physically wipe away your tears. As I sit today, God hovers over those parts of my story that have become disordered by tragedy, death, sin, or violence. As I grieve in lament over these areas, I no longer feel alone or like I will drown. Somehow, I can sit in the truth of my circumstances and the truth of God's good character—holding and feeling the weight of each.

It's not supposed to be this way, friend, and it won't always be.

CHAPTER SIX

WHAT'S IN A NAME?

GENESIS 1:14–25 {DAYS FOUR AND FIVE}

THIS IS MY FATHER'S WORLD:
I REST ME IN THE THOUGHT
OF ROCKS AND TREES, OF SKIES AND SEAS;
HIS HAND THE WONDERS WROUGHT.

After Clara was diagnosed with cancer, we stayed in the hospital for two weeks while she recovered from a major surgery and started radiation and chemotherapy. In those short weeks, she went from seemingly healthy to incredibly fragile—losing her hair, 10 percent of her body weight, and even height from the radiation to her spine.

When it was time for treatment to continue from home, the hospital nurses sat me down with a binder full of information and bags of medicines, special toys, lotions, supplements, and more. This binder was unbelievable. It was one of those five-inch-thick ones with tabs and folders. There was a spot for recording blood-work numbers and tabs for different chemotherapies with their particular makeup and side effects. There were sections with resources, and sections for physical therapy and occupational therapy.

As we signed the discharge papers, it felt like when we took Stephen home as first-time parents. Once again, we were holding a fragile life in our hands, totally inexperienced and overwhelmed. I did not feel up to the enormous task ahead of us; somehow, the nurses and doctors thought we could manage. It was the first time I doubted their judgment and thought an educated professional should always accompany the Big C Binder.

When we got home, I unloaded the binder, the bag full of prescriptions, and the bag full of all our new medical equipment and tools. My mom took one look at it spread across the kitchen table and declared that we needed a cabinet.

We purchased a small black cabinet, and in went the binder and medicines and the endless grab bag of treatments and gear. I dubbed it the "Cancer Cabinet" and was grateful for its organization. The cabinet was our go-to for all things cancer-related during her six months of treatment.

About a year after Clara's full recovery, the Cancer Cabinet stood empty. My instinct was to throw it away because of its painful association, but that seemed wasteful. Instead, we repurposed it to hold the kids' electronics. We called it the "Charging Cabinet." Apparently, we like alliteration.

A cancer cabinet and a charging cabinet are two very different things, even though the piece of furniture is the same. The name I gave the little black cabinet clarifies its purpose. As we look at days four and five in the creation story, we'll see that the names given to parts of nature play a key role in cosmogonies. We use names to give clarity, like the name of a textbook or a novel, and the ancient Israelites utilized names to designate purpose.

The reason something exists is important to us, but remember, purpose was the primary focus for the ancient Israelites and their neighbors when they swapped creation stories. The way they would assign purpose to something was to give it a name.[1]

NAMES ARE A BIG DEAL

As we are eavesdropping and God is introducing Himself to His people, He's going to speak to them in ways they are ready to hear. They are listening for the purpose or the *why* of creation, and names are a vehicle for answering that question.

The word *cabinet* didn't completely describe the function of our piece of furniture until we named it the Cancer Cabinet or the Charging Cabinet. Similarly, names were also a big deal to Israel's neighboring cultures. Remember our Mesopotamian text, *Enuma Elish?* The opening lines describe chaos as, "When on high no name was given to heaven / Nor below was the netherworld called by name."[2] Names were so important to the diverse cultures of the ANE (including in this Babylonian story) that the description of chaos was that things were nameless. The lack of a name signaled that things were out of order and needed to be put in their place. An important part of cosmogonies, or creation texts, is that they were interested in objects' names because the name clarified *why* the object was there.[3]

A clear example of the naming principle is when God separates the light from the dark and then He names them.[4] The light is called "day," and the dark is named "night."

Then God said, "Let there be light," and there was light. And God saw that the light was good. Then he separated the light from the darkness. God called the light "day" and the darkness "night." And evening passed and morning came, marking the first day. (Gen. 1:3–5 NLT)

If you were thinking about these verses with the mindset of an ancient Israelite, you would say, "I get it. The purpose of the light is for the day, and the purpose of the darkness is for the night."

It was not that the word *day* replaced the word *light*. There were still two different words—light and day. Rather, the way God names the day and the night explains their purpose to the Israelites. God says the light's purpose is to mark the day; the darkness's purpose is to mark the night.

A LITTLE ANCIENT HISTORY

Israel's neighboring cultures went one step further when naming and designating a purpose within creation stories. When they assigned a name to a part of nature, that name would sometimes be the name of a god because that god was in charge of that area. This is unusual to those of us who have only been around the Genesis account of creation. A little exposure to other ancient cosmogonies can demonstrate how deities found their place in a creation story. Let's look again at the Babylonian text *Enuma Elish* to see how this played out.

As a brief reminder, *Enuma Elish*'s plot started with chaos, moved to gods fighting, and then the winning god, Marduk, put the other gods in place (for a little more history of *Enuma Elish*, flip back to chapter 3). In this part of the passage, Marduk is doing his super-god thing and organizing the universe. Below is a passage that describes how Marduk went about his job. (The "he" in this passage is Marduk.) When you read it, pretend there are travelers gathered around a campfire, and a friendly older grandmother is telling this story as you gaze up to the sky.

He made the position(s) for the great gods,
He established (in) constellations the stars, their likenesses.
He marked the year, described its boundaries,
He set up twelve months of three stars each
After he had patterned the days of the year,
He fixed the position of Neberu to mark the (stars')
    relationships.
Lest any make an error or go astray,
He established the position(s) of Enlil and Ea in relation to it.[5]

Poetic, no? Let me point out a few things to you that were normal to the ancient reader but may escape our notice.

JOB ASSIGNMENTS

Marduk doesn't actually make anything, does he? He's putting things into place that already are in existence. This was pretty normal in ancient cosmogonies. Many gods existed when the stories started, and the winning god gave them an assigned job after the battle.

NAMES

Did you see the names? Neberu is the god of the passage, likely what we know as the Milky Way. Enlil is the god of the atmosphere, and Ea is the god of subterranean fresh water and wisdom.

So why did ANE cultures identify parts of nature with gods? Recall that the religious orientation of the ancient world was polytheism or many gods. Picture it like a wealthy patriarch who set up a large household and put sons in charge of different areas. The sons hired employees to oversee smaller pieces.[6] It was a delegation designed to account for every little thing.

In a household, it would look something like this:

> Here are the wheat crops; Baker runs that section.
> Here's the household manager; Marshall is responsible for
>   ensuring it runs well.
> Here's the sheep; Shepherd keeps them safe and sound.

In the religious pantheon, it would look a bit like this:

> Here's the freshwater, Ea.
> Here's the Milky Way, Neberu.

The name tells you the function but also specifies who is in charge of that area. The god gets the credit when things go well, and they also get an appeal when things are falling apart.

> Got a problem with the stars? Take it up with Neberu.
> Has fresh water been a help to you? Make sure to thank Ea.

Though a different worldview from ours, it was the norm for ANE cultures to integrate elements of nature thoughtfully and theologically into their religion. For example, most ancient cultures viewed the sun as a god of justice.[7] They drew a relationship between the sun bringing light to what was hidden and the concept of justice. When listening to a creation account, the ancient cultures would not have flinched when an object was given a name that was expected to correspond with a deity.

GENESIS

Back to our campfire, where the Israelite takes his turn to tell the Genesis account. Again, picture yourself tired but with a full belly and a beautiful clear night to capture your gaze as you lean over shoulders to eavesdrop. A grandfather tells this story well:

> Then God said, "Let lights appear in the sky to separate the day from the night. Let them be signs to mark the seasons, days, and years. Let these lights in the sky shine down on the earth." And that is what happened. God made two great lights—the larger one to govern the day, and the smaller one to govern the night. He also made the stars. God set these lights in the sky to light the earth, to govern the day and night, and to separate the light from the darkness. And God saw that it was good.
>
> And evening passed and morning came, marking the fourth day.
>
> Then God said, "Let the waters swarm with fish and other life. Let the skies be filled with birds of every kind." So God created great sea creatures and every living thing that scurries and swarms in the water, and every sort of bird—each producing offspring of the same kind. And God saw that it was good. Then God blessed them, saying, "Be fruitful and multiply. Let the fish fill the seas, and let the birds multiply on the earth."
>
> And evening passed and morning came, marking the fifth day.
>
> Then God said, "Let the earth produce every sort of animal, each producing offspring of the same kind—livestock, small animals that scurry along the ground, and wild animals." And that is what happened. God made all sorts of wild animals, livestock, and small animals, each able to produce offspring of the same kind. And God saw that it was good. (Gen. 1:14–25 NLT)

By now, you're starting to see some of the things that were part of the norm within this cosmogony literature, and you're also starting to see a few things that stuck out as a bit different from the other creation stories.

Let's start with the normal.

PURPOSE DESCRIBED

We see what God does, and then we see why He does it. Allow me a chart to visually represent Genesis 1:14–18. The left side is what God did—and our twenty-first-century worldview is drawn to that left side. When we heard this story in Sunday school, the chart's left side was probably the part our teacher emphasized.

But remember, we are eavesdropping! So, as we read through the text again, it's central to remember that the cultures across the ANE were interested in the chart's right side. They would say, "God made the sun and the moon—great! But what is it *for?*"

WHAT God Did	WHY He Did It
¹⁴ Then God said:	
"Let lights appear in the sky	to separate the day from the night.
	Let them be signs to mark the seasons, days, and years.
	¹⁵ Let these lights in the sky shine down on the earth."
And that is what happened.	
¹⁶ God made two great lights—	the larger one to govern the day
	and the smaller one to govern the night.

He also made the stars.	
	[17] God set these lights in the sky to light the earth,
	[18] to govern the day and night,
	and to separate the light from the darkness.
And God saw it was good.	

This pattern of stating what God did and then explaining why He did it (or what the purpose for it was) is really familiar. As we've seen, God doesn't have an issue with the ANE style of communication—He uses it as a way to tell them what's important to Him.

Around that campfire, as a grandfather tells about God making the universe, what details (or lack of details) would have intrigued the ANE listeners? Where would they lean in, where would they nod, and where would they furrow their brow?

CREATE FIRST, ASSIGN SECOND

God made the sun and the moon and the stars. This is weird. Not *super* odd, but it's definitely out of the ordinary. As we've discussed, ANE cultures thought the sun and the moon were gods. In fact, they were big deal gods.[8] In Egypt and Mesopotamia, the sun plays an essential role in all three of their creation accounts. To Egyptians, "the most important element in their cosmological scheme was the sun (the god Re)."[9] It was so important that their world couldn't function without it.

When God says He made the sun and the moon and the stars, He lowered their status. They were demoted from a preexisting god to something God made. This declaration would have been curious, at the least, and, at the most, offensive.

God gave the Israelites a very clear picture of the universe and how it was designed to run, and He created each object to function within its allotted place. He did not delegate a sun god to run the daytime; He put the sun in the sky to mark seasons, days, and years. God did not allot His authority to anyone else to run what He created; He remained actively in charge.

We saw the sun was thought to be a god of justice in ANE cultures. When God made the sun an object He created, He also claimed the sun god's function.[10] Justice was not handed out to a different deity but handled directly by an involved Creator.[11] If the people had concerns about seasons or weather, they weren't to seek help from the sun god but from Yahweh. Likewise, if there was anxiety about justice, Yahweh was the involved Creator who would address their concerns.

NO NAMES

Where are the names of the sun and the moon? When you read that God put in place greater and lesser lights to govern the day and the evening, you probably understood that to be the sun and moon. Did you wonder why they weren't named "sun" and "moon"? There was a Hebrew word for each, so why did God carefully steer clear of naming them?

When God left the moon and the sun nameless, He avoided any chance that they would be understood as gods.[12] Around the campfire, this would have stopped those from Mesopotamia or Egypt in their tracks. It's as if God created a position in a household and then left the job vacant! The ANE audience would be whispering and sputtering that something was wrong. They would wonder how the moon could operate as an object, a lesser light, and not as a deity. God's very simple and intentional omission of a name would have had the men and women from ANE cultures reeling.

As an eavesdropper, this is where we need to lean in hard. If something set the ancient campfire audience buzzing, we'd be foolish not to seek out some understanding. God has delivered some pretty intense theological game changers.

God made a very bold move and transferred the sun, moon, and stars into the category of made stuff. They did not have any power in themselves. The sun was presented a little like a Roomba (those robot vacuums). It was a powerful tool that did what God said, when God said it, for the purpose God had ordained. The sun and the moon's only purpose was to light the day and the evening and to set up the seasons and years under God's direction. God completely restructured the hierarchical organization of the universe in this straightforward proclamation: "God made the two great lights, the greater light to govern the day, and the lesser light to govern the night; he made the stars also" (Gen. 1:16 NLT).

Because the universe's organization was woven tightly with how the varied cultures of the ANE understood the spiritual purpose of gods, God also dismantled their understanding of religion. He cleared out the religious house without any warfare or mighty power. He simply stated they never were gods in the first place. He recategorized them.

God was planting a seed of monotheism in the many-god ANE cultures. He was telling them He had power and control, asking them to worship and depend on Him alone.

Yeah, that would make a campfire buzz.

In my mind's eye, I picture the older folks at the campfire leaning back and crossing their arms and the younger ones leaning in, curious and open. I don't know about you, but the older I get, the less likely I am to greet theological game changers with open arms. I've been comfortable with my understanding of who God is for a while, and it irritates me a bit when I need to expand my theology. And I've found that the more invested I am in my position, the harder it is for me to let God broaden my viewpoints. Remembering that I can trust God lets me relax my posture when He teaches me something new from His Word or convicts me about some things I need to change.

A MESSAGE TO ISRAEL

Allegiance to Yahweh wasn't a pointed message for Israel's neighbors. God was talking to Israel when He didn't say the Hebrew word for sun. This particular area was a trouble spot for the Israelites. There is a name for the sun in Hebrew; it's *šemeš* (pronounced SHEH-mesh). The Assyrian and Babylonian name for the sun god was Shamash. Phonetically, the word sun was similar because their language had similar origins.

God's biggest concern was not phonetics. Phonetics simply highlighted the problem. The Israelites were not great about avoiding worshiping their neighbors' gods, and the sun god was no exception. It was such a problem for Israel that God made an explicit command that they shouldn't worship the sun, "and when you look up into the sky and see the sun, moon, and stars—all the forces of heaven—don't be seduced into worshiping them. The LORD your God gave them to all the peoples of the earth" (Deut. 4:19 NLT).

Unfortunately, the Israelites did not obey that commandment. Sun worship pops up all across the Old Testament, from Job to Ezekiel.[13] God said through His prophet Jeremiah, "The sun, moon, and stars—the gods my people have loved, served, and worshiped" (Jer. 8:2a NLT).

Perhaps Israel worshiped the sun because they struggled to resist a larger cultural norm. God was asking them to think about religion in a way that was completely different from any other cultures in their world, asking them to behave contrary to their natural default. Or perhaps the Israelites were drawn to the sun as a powerful visual they could see impacting their agricultural society. Or maybe they longed for justice and wondered if the sun could provide it. For whatever reason, Israel turned to the gods of their neighbors and worshiped them, the sun god in particular.

It's important to note that the Israelites were not worshiping the sun god *instead* of worshiping God. They were worshiping the sun god in *addition* to worshiping God. We naturally think about religion as something you have or don't have, one you choose and one you reject. The Israelites weren't hopping from one god to another. To cultures that only thought about worship within a larger hierarchy, it would have been natural to add a sun god into the worship they were already aligned with.

But God rejected the sun as a god and specifically warned His people not to worship it. A few chapters later in Deuteronomy, He called on them to worship Him exclusively, "Listen, O Israel! The LORD is our God, the LORD alone. And you must love the LORD your God with all your heart, all your soul, and all your strength" (Deut. 6:4–5 NLT).

The reality God describes in creation says that He has not delegated His authority. If the ANE cultures were inclined to think of the sun as a god of justice, God was saying *He* is justice, not Shamash. God unequivocally stated that all appeals and all praise must go to one God, a God actively involved in His creation.

Dr. Richard Averbeck, professor of Old Testament and Semitic Languages at Trinity Evangelical Divinity School, says that Genesis 1–11 "presents Yahweh as the one true God who stands above and outside of both the world and history. He created the world from outside of it and still stands in that transcendent position even within history."[14]

A MESSAGE FOR US

Since I don't make offerings to the sun or look to it for justice, I'm good here, right? Not really, because false worship is not just about the sun. Jesus warned about divided worship and affection in His most famous sermon, the Sermon on the Mount. And he didn't poke the listeners about the sun god, He talked about money. "No one can serve two masters. For you will hate one and love the other; you will be devoted to one and despise the other. You cannot serve God and be enslaved to money" (Matt. 6:24 NLT).

Money is just a different sun god slipping into a pantheon.

When I elevate something beyond its God-given design or purpose, I have been seduced into dividing my heart. It's not like I completely abandon God in favor of money, bowing down to my bank accounts and making altars to the economy. Rather, I simply add it to my list of things I have to manage. In time, it creeps up in importance, and before I know it, a bit of my heart has pledged allegiance to the dollar. I trust our bank accounts for our provision, forgetting God reigns over our dollars too.

As is the case with all biblical teaching, the principle underneath the specifics preaches to us today. In the Old Testament, God tells His people not to serve the sun god because God alone is responsible for creation (and justice). In the New Testament, Jesus tells us not to serve money because money is a created thing. God alone is responsible for our well-being. From the beginning, God has been telling humanity that we are a people apt to divide our loyalties and hearts.

Examining our fears is an excellent indicator to show where we have misplaced trust. Fear is a flag that waves over what we hold most precious, the thing we are most alarmed to lose, the source of our restless hearts. If we look at what we've been most angry, frustrated, or fearful about over the last year, we will see something that has elevated itself (with our ignorant permission) to a status it doesn't deserve. I've certainly done it.

When I was afraid a disease was limiting me—*that flag of fear was waving over the god of my health.*

When we were afraid all our savings were lost—*that flag of fear was flying over the god of self-sufficiency.*

When I was afraid of a political party gaining control—*that flag of fear was waving over the god of my security.*

So, what have I done when I am afraid or restless? Unfortunately, it's often the same thing the ancient Israelites did when their crops failed, or an enemy threatened to destroy them. I appealed to my resources for help. I tightened up my control. I worked and strived within what I knew.

When the things we care about are threatened, our initial reactions tell us a lot. I was devastated on a Wednesday morning in November of an election year. My husband met me in the kitchen that morning and told me the results of a contentious election, and I felt like a rug had been pulled out from under me. We quietly made our coffee and breakfast and stared in the distance. I wasn't just disappointed, and I wasn't simply frustrated. I was devastated—and my intense response made me realize I had placed my hope and trust in the government. Now that the government I understood was changing, my hopes were crushed. And I was afraid.

In hindsight, I can see that the fear of an undesirable political party gaining control waved over the god of my personal security, so I clenched my fist tight around information and became preoccupied with the news.

Whatever is in that closed hand is what we will fiercely and instinctively protect. We seek control just as the ancient Israelites did. They sought it out by appealing to a sun god; they gave it credit for life and order and appealed to it for help when things went wrong. We preserve what we serve by exercising control and clenching that fist tightly. When life flows as we feel it should, we give our efforts and good works the credit for life and order. When things fall apart, we appeal to our grit, enter straight-up denial, or change our circumstances. It's a desperate attempt to regain an emotional equilibrium and to silence our fears.

As our hearts divide and our loyalties split, the God of creation doesn't fight what we allowed to sneak into our pantheon. God is not intimidated by our false gods and their ability to impact our lives. He's not combatting a sun god; He's warning about our divided hearts.

God will not fit into the segments we carve out. It's all or nothing. We can't serve two masters. With clarity and unambiguous language, God will call out what we are serving. He has defined how our relationship with Him will work, and He will not move pieces around in the religious structures we set up.

From my reaction on that Wednesday morning, I learned that my hopes were caught up in an election. I would not have known it (and indeed would have honestly denied it) until the unfavorable results hit my gut that morning. My fears waved over the god of my dependence on the government for personal security, and until God let me see it, I served it. It had snuck into my pantheon, and I didn't even know it was there.

We are called to love the Lord with a singular heart and to serve Him alone. Following God's command means we need an awareness that we are apt to divide our hearts and try to serve two masters. It means that with humble conviction, we open our hands that are tightly gripping our mini gods. God calls us to prayerfully repent, dump the exposed treasures, and then deliberately fill those empty hands up with God. The battleground is in our hearts; the fight is for our allegiance.

Creation teaches us that our default is to find ways to control our circumstances, and creation invites us to change our default to trust.

If God was switching the narrative on the Israelites to think of the sun as a greater light and the moon as a lesser light, what if we did the same with our false gods, such as money or health, independence or security? Or with anything that may seduce us? How about reframing our thoughts and focusing on the *purpose* those objects serve under God's reign so that we don't let created things reign over us?

Maybe we call money our "lesser coin," remembering God reigns over our provision. Or our health is our "service fuel," and we recall God is our breath and life and being (Acts 17:28). And our government is our "policymaker," accountable to a God who sits on the throne. Somehow, when we rename things and remember God is an involved Creator, it can change our association or highlight its purpose in our lives, like a cancer cabinet becoming a charging cabinet.

God told the ancient Israelites that there was no purpose

for the sun in their lives beyond what He had told the sun to do (to light the day and mark the seasons). God says the same to us. There is no purpose for anything beyond the purpose God designed it to have. So, open your hands, friend. Have the courage to see what is hidden in your palm and prayerfully ask God to help you expose it, drop it, and let your open hands trust Him.

And then do it again tomorrow.

CHAPTER SEVEN

MADE IN THE IMAGE

GENESIS 1:26–31 {DAY SIX}

THIS IS MY FATHER'S WORLD,
THE BIRDS THEIR CAROLS RAISE,
THE MORNING LIGHT, THE LILY WHITE,
DECLARE THEIR MAKER'S PRAISE.

I started my college career as an elementary education major. My mom taught third grade, and I was pretty good with kids, so it seemed like the right path for me. Fortunately, the program I entered insisted on putting college freshmen into elementary-aged classrooms as soon as possible. After thirty minutes of watching a teacher wrangle an overpopulated room full of first graders, I knew I had chosen the wrong career.

Within a few semesters, I switched to child psychology. It was fascinating. I loved learning how brains developed, how kids communicated, and how they each responded differently to the same stimuli. I loved the challenge of understanding them. And I especially loved that it could be done in a quiet room without thirty other kids hollering for a snack.

One of my favorite things I learned in my new major was the

psychology of family portraits. A child will unknowingly give us insight into their view of the world by how they draw their family. With their fists clutched around a crayon, the little drawings end up telling on them. For example, see the picture my niece Lucy drew of her family.

Looking at the picture, we might ask if Lucy drew herself small or big. Is she with her family or off to the side? The child who feels her household is a cohesive unit will draw herself as a part of the whole, as Lucy did here (she's in the middle of the five kids). Similarly, a child might draw herself small if she feels she doesn't have a valuable role to play. Each child allows their environment to inform their purpose, standing, and value. You and I do the same thing as adults—however, unconsciously.

After I graduated and had kids, I fell into the overanalyzing trap that many psychology students do and would fixate on my kids' drawings. I'd obsess over where they placed themselves in the picture and try to ask nonchalant questions about their illustration choices. You should know I've never been nonchalant in my life, so my poor kids probably felt like it was an inquisition when they pulled out their kindergarten take-home folder. Also, I should add that drawings aren't always a direct line into kids' perspectives about their family dynamics. Sometimes, kids draw themselves little in the corner because they are depicting themselves like a mouse stealing a cookie, not because they feel small and isolated. I had to learn to think in broad strokes about this stuff.

PURPOSE

We know how Western children might draw their families, but what about children in ANE cultures? They would likely start with a picture that included themselves inside a larger family unit, possibly involving their parents, grandparents, aunts and uncles, and cousins. It was probable they lived in a house with many additions that included these family members.[1] Their lives were intricately intertwined with their extended family.

When it comes to daily life, Western children might include chores, headphones, or computers; children in ANE cultures would undoubtedly include the land they lived and farmed. And worth noting, they most likely would have included the king and gods in their pictures. Gods and kings would have been a presence looming large in their lives, filling their conversations and directing their activities (perhaps a kindergarten teacher would be akin to this type of presence in a five-year-old's life).

A child in ANE cultures would know her family farmed the land for their own provision but also that her grandfather, as the head of their household, sent products of their farming up to the king. The king would then use it and redistribute it as necessary, often serving as head priest, ensuring the gods were fed by leaving them offerings. This is how her world was set up, and it worked well for thousands of years.

I asked my niece Lucy to imagine she was a child in an ANE culture and draw a picture of her ANE family. Her dad happens to have an ANE PhD, so he helped her out. Here's what she drew. Note they are living with extended family and workers on a farm. There is a road leading from their farm to the king's home. She also drew an altar in front of their home (see Judg. 6:25–26).

The picture also depicts how Lucy, if she were an ANE child, would have fit into the world, a world founded on her relationship with her gods. Remember, in ANE cultures, there was no such thing as a godless or even god-uninvolved society. Looking at this example picture can tell us how she felt about her home, but more importantly, how she understood the gods to view *her*. At an early age, she would have known who her gods were and her purpose in relation to them.

As we've learned, cosmogonies are about the formation of the universe. But remember, these stories were also answering questions of purpose, not process. They tell what the gods were like and how humanity was to operate within that cosmos. Understanding how society and homes were run can help us understand cosmogonies because cosmogonies echo the household structure. The running of a home was the working out of their theology or belief about where they belonged in the world. Deep questions like, "What is my purpose?" were answered within cosmogonies. Let's look at a few and see how people and their purpose are depicted.

I GET BY WITH A LITTLE HELP

Enki and Ninmah

Humanity has an interesting beginning in the Sumerian story *Enki and Ninmah.* In this cosmogony, the lesser gods were laboring and frustrated at their workload. They complained as they dug irrigation canals for agriculture, smashing their equipment. To solve the problem, Enki instructs Nammu to use clay and within a goddess to form and birth humanity. Once humankind is formed, Enki declares that humanity will then carry the burden of other gods:

> And when Enki, the-fashioner-of-the-forms,
> pondered by himself their nature,
> He said to his mother, Nammu:
> "My mother, the creature which you named,[2]
> will verily exist; impose (on him)
> the burden of the gods!"[3]

Problem solved! Humanity was created for the express purpose of alleviating the burden of the gods.

Atra-hasis

The Babylonian story of *Atra-hasis* has a similar trajectory to *Enki and Ninmah*. In *Atra-hasis*, the lesser gods performed forced labor, digging canals and wells. The lesser gods burned their tools and went to the gods in charge, demanding a change. In response, the gods formed man from clay and the blood and flesh of a slaughtered god.

In both the Babylonian and Sumerian accounts, humanity was created to ease the burden of the gods.[4] And this wasn't necessarily a negative thing! To the people of ANE cultures, this was a great privilege and honor. There was dignity in their assignment and value placed on their role within creation. Humanity was the solution to a problem, an aid to deities.

Merikare

There is a similar concept in Egyptian accounts. *Merikare* is an Egyptian text of instruction from a king to his son that ends with a hymn to the creator god. This hymn has pieces of cosmogony, giving us insight into how Egyptians saw their purpose in the world. It is quite fitting to include a bit of cosmogony within the instruction genre, just as you or I might include a prayer of praise after offering words of guidance to our children.

Take a look at a few of the lines:

> Work for god, he will work for you also,
> With offerings that make the altar flourish,
> With carvings that proclaim your name,
> God thinks of him who works for him.[5]

The best way Pharoah, an Egyptian king, could succeed was to remember his place and his purpose. He was to work for the gods and give them offerings.[6]

OUR PLACE IN THE WORLD

The following grid is a handy summary of how many men and women across varied ANE cultures viewed their position in the world.

ANE Household Model[7]
Gods = true landowners
King = land supervisor
Families = land workers

The gods created and owned everything they ordered. Over that creation, they set up kings to serve as rulers of the land and priests of the gods' temples in their appointed cities. The rest of humanity was honored to serve the king and gods with the works of their hands.

GENESIS

Genesis, however, has a different perspective.

In Genesis, day six started by filling up the land formed on day three. Living creatures and beasts and everything that creeps were made, and God saw that it was good (Gen. 1:24–25). Then God made humanity:

Then God said, "Let Us make man in Our image, according to Our likeness; and let them rule over the fish of the sea and over the birds of the sky and over the cattle and over all the earth, and over every creeping thing that creeps on the earth." God created man in His own image, in the image of God He created him; male and female He created them. (Gen. 1:26–27)

If we're sitting around an ANE campfire, listening as our favorite storyteller is reciting Genesis to fellow shepherds, I imagine that he would make a theatrical presentation of verses 26 and 27. After all, humanity was being presented in an unusual light. Now, remember, we are eavesdropping on an ancient conversation. What was unusual for them may not be for us. So, we need to see it from their perspective in order to grasp the full revelation of what was happening. And good stuff was happening.

First, did you notice that God didn't make humanity as workers to ease His burdens? God doesn't demonstrate weariness because of His workload or frustration at the earth. Creation of humanity was a part of God's very good creation—a piece of the already functioning ecosystem. We aren't an afterthought made to fix a problem in God's world.

Second, did you see the repeated phrase "image of God"? If you're like me, I always pictured this to say that God looked just like us but lots bigger (a little like a blimp, to be honest). But that's not quite the full gist of the ANE understanding for this phrase. To the man or woman within the diverse ANE cultures, the phrase "image of God" was one reserved for idols, kings, and other deities.[8]

IMAGE OF GOD: ṢELEM PROVIDED FOR

The Hebrew word for *image* in Genesis 1:26 is *ṣelem* (pronounced *TSEH-lem*), a word often translated as *idol*.[9] Across the ANE, idols were more than statues acting as representations of gods. Priests gave idols "offerings of food, drink, clothing, and shelter (in the temple)," believing they were "a *physical, living manifestation* of an otherwise invisible reality."[10]

Notice how God flips the ANE cultural script in Genesis. Instead of humanity creating a divine *ṣelem* and then providing food and shelter for that *ṣelem*, *God made humanity* to be a *ṣelem* (as a representative) and *provided for humanity* a place to dwell and food to eat. He did not need creation to sustain Him. In fact, all throughout the religious activity of the Old and New Testaments, God never relied on humanity to provide for Him.

> Then God said, "Behold, I have given you every plant yielding seed that is on the surface of all the earth, and every tree which has fruit yielding seed; it shall be food for you; and to every beast of the earth and to every bird of the sky and to everything that moves on the earth which has life, I have given every green plant for food"; and it was so. (Gen. 1:29–30)

God's perfect design had provision for humanity and animals built into the setup. Creation didn't have a place for hunger. When God sat on His throne to reign, it was over a system with every need covered. It is in His character to create good things and to sustain His creation (more on this in chapter 10).

Far more than the gods of ANE cultures,[11] God repeatedly tells *us* to depend on *Him* for provision throughout Scripture (Ps. 145:15–16 and Matt. 6:31–32 are two passages among many). His character is consistent on this throughout the Bible, but for whatever reason, I often struggle to believe that it is in God's character to make sure I have enough. My go-to is to fret, worry, and live from a position of self-reliance. Unfortunately, the fruit of that mindset is pride, anxiety, and self-protection; generosity takes a back seat, and joy takes a long vacation. It's silly sometimes to realize I'm worrying as I take a long walk, breathing in the air perfectly designed for my lungs. God has already provided abundantly, and His regular and dependable provision slips into my mental background.

Yet, living in the reality that God is a provider is really hard when something like unemployment hits. Our foggy day seven means brokenness in our reality. Sometimes, the pantry looks bare, and we don't have enough gas money. Scripture doesn't ignore that this happens or how we may struggle. The book of Genesis jumps right into the issue when Abraham faces a famine and treks all the way across Canaan to find food. And Jesus knows we can feel like we don't have enough because He addressed it directly:

> "That is why I tell you not to worry about everyday life—whether you have enough food and drink, or enough clothes to wear. Isn't life more than food, and your body more than clothing? Look at the birds. They don't plant or harvest or store food in barns, for your heavenly Father feeds them. And aren't you far more valuable to him than they are? Can all your worries add a single moment to your life?
>
> "And why worry about your clothing? Look at the lilies of the field and how they grow. They don't work or make their clothing, yet Solomon in all his glory was not dressed as beautifully as they are. And if God cares so wonderfully for wildflowers that are here today and thrown into the fire tomorrow, he will certainly care for you. Why do you have so little faith?
>
> "So don't worry about these things, saying, 'What will we

eat? What will we drink? What will we wear?' These things dominate the thoughts of unbelievers, but your heavenly Father already knows all your needs. Seek the Kingdom of God above all else, and live righteously, and he will give you everything you need.

"So don't worry about tomorrow, for tomorrow will bring its own worries. Today's trouble is enough for today." (Matt. 6:25–34 NLT)

When the knot hits our stomachs because we realize we can't cover our bills, Jesus encourages us to look at creation and remember Him as the Creator. Just like in Genesis 1, He says we can trust Him to provide. Keeping our eyes on who He is amid brokenness and suffering is where the rubber meets the road, and the area of provision is no exception. Goodness knows this one is hard, because we are called to live sacrificially (Eph. 5:1–2) and life will involve suffering (Matt. 16:24–26). But God doesn't tell us to just get over it. There is sweet relief available in Jesus' invitation to take it one day at a time and focus on Him while the flowers and sparrows stand as witnesses.

And here's the disclaimer: I'm not suggesting God doesn't ask us to work hard—He does. And, of course, we are called to employment as a means to support our families. But our provision—in seasons of both plenty and want—is not because we worked hard. We are provided for because God cares for His creation *and* we act as stewards in partnership with Him. Our work is a way to steward the bodies, minds, and energy God has given us. We work as a way to participate in God's redemptive story, through service and joy. Paychecks and grocery money and the harvest all come from God as His provision.

King David's prayer has become a helpful touchstone to remind me that everything I possess is from God. After the people of Israel gave a generous offering for the construction of the temple, King David said to God, "But who am I, and who are my people, that we could give anything to you? Everything we have has come from you, and we give you only what you first gave us!" (1 Chron. 29:14 NLT). Paul says something similar in Acts when preaching, "For in him we live and move and have our being" (Acts 17:28 NIV).

After I do well at my work, cook a good meal, have a great conversation, or handle something strategically, I silently pray, "Thank You for the provision." Any success I have is an outpouring of God's provision combined with my best efforts at stewardship; it's a dual effort. The problem is when I take all the credit, acting as if I have created myself and my environment. God gave first because God is a generous provider.

IMAGE OF GOD: KING

In the ANE, the phrase "image of God" also referred to kings because the gods ruled the world through their appointed king. As Dr. Bernard Batto, a specialist in the Hebrew Bible within its cultural and historical context, says, the "human king was the 'image' of the divine sovereign, his viceroy on earth, charged with perfecting the divine sovereign's work of creation by promoting right order, justice, and the human weal [well-being]."[12]

Remember that across the diverse cultures of ANE households, the common man was a land worker. He eased the burden of the gods by working the land. He also had the honor of providing food and sustenance to the gods via the products of the land he sent to the image of god, the king. As an image of god, the king would govern and lead as a representation of that god. He imparted the values and precepts that were important to the gods.[13]

Now slip back to the campfire and listen as a grandfather says that humanity—everyone around that campfire—is made in the image of God. This was an incredible claim. As Dr. Batto states, "Kingship has been democratized. Not just kings but all humans bear this royal badge of divinity."[14]

Creation Model
Yahweh = True landowner
Families (image of God) = Land supervisor *and* land worker

This kingship democratization is astounding. God said that every occupation, from the farmer to the potter to the seamstress, was working as a king. It's as true today of the teacher, the executive, the janitor, the stay-at-home mom, and the insurance salesman.

Stand up a little straighter, friend, because God says your work is as worthwhile as royalty! You are not inconsequential; you are significant! Your role is important, and your interactions have consequence. The Creator of the universe has determined that you are important and has imbued you with the power to act for the betterment of His creation.

But also, as you stand a little straighter, you may tremble a bit. This role is important, and it has consequences. There is no escaping your role as an image of God when you stop at the market for some ice cream. You will always represent a trustworthy Creator.

When God made every human in His image, He gave each of us great value and great responsibility. Everywhere we go, we represent God. You and I have been given the privilege and responsibility to act as representatives of His character, and our interactions make a difference and have significance.

And did you catch that both men and women are made in God's image? As far as I have discovered, Genesis is the only creation account to specifically include both genders. Men and women, working in community and tandem, are acting in God's image. So not only do our interactions have responsibility and privilege, but our actions with our friends, family, church, and neighbors are to be representative.

Did my friend and I fight when we got out of the car, calling each other names and making digs at each other? Was I giving my husband the silent treatment all through the checkout, making everyone feel the icy separation between us? Did our messy family leave our trash at our table as we left the restaurant without consideration for the people coming behind us? How we act as a group and community is part of being an image bearer.

In other words, this is not a solo gig. We are *all* made in God's image. How I treat you and how you treat me reflects our theology. When I show bias, I act as if God made us differently, endowing some with more value than others. My actions tell those around me that I feel God made Susie best, but Jenny was made pretty good.

Just as hunger wasn't in the creation account, there also is no place for racism, sexism, classism, partiality, favoritism, or any value differential between people. When we feel these relational and power-driven chasms, they are a result of our fallen world, not a part of God's design.

Here's my second disclaimer: we have lots of different things to consider in our relationships at home and work, essential distinctions like boundaries and safety and wisdom. There may be significant lines in the sand we draw inside our spheres, but be sure not to slip into a value judgment on that person we're protecting ourselves from. They are made in the image of God, just as we are. Additionally, sometimes hierarchies exist as helpful organizational structures. They aren't all rife with isms. It's not the structure that's a problem; it's when the top-down structure becomes a top-down value judgment. We are not better or worse than anyone else.

This one is a fight, friend. Our minds have equated worth with position since the line leader was chosen in kindergarten. We will slip into making value determinations about a person based on their driving skills, political choices, sexual orientation, or career. Our thoughts and actions are like little pictures we draw about how we see the world. They will tell on us. Sometimes, as an experiment, I check my internal dialogue about someone I respect. Do I subtly elevate their value to be higher than yours or others'? Or how do I feel about people I am frustrated with? I sometimes say some pretty belittling things in my head as I wait in line at the gas station. It creeps up on us!

If we aren't careful, our environment will determine our purpose, standing, and value. Sometimes, that same environment inadvertently determines our neighbors' purpose, standing, or value. It's good to plant a stake in the ground and let creation teach us how God views us and how He views others. As an image of God, He provides for us and bestows remarkable privilege and responsibility to us. What an extraordinary statement God made in creation! The next logical question is *how* are we to act as God's ambassadors, His image? That will be the subject of our next chapter.

CHAPTER EIGHT

RESTORATION PARTICIPATION

GENESIS 1:26–31 {DAY SIX}

MY GRACIOUS MASTER AND MY GOD,
ASSIST ME TO PROCLAIM,
TO SPREAD THROUGH ALL THE EARTH ABROAD
THE HONORS OF YOUR NAME.

I was a little irritated at the tattling that was happening in my house. It was impossible to get anything done with all the "she did this" and "he did that" interruptions that were bombarding me from all directions. In early elementary school, Stephen was particularly sensitive to the injustices he saw. He was constantly coming up to me and pointing out things he viewed as unfair and pressuring me to make them right.

I decided we needed a change in perspective, so I called him over one day and explained that he had a new job. He was going to be the household "grace police." Every time he saw something that was wrong or felt like he had been overlooked, he had an opportunity to hand out grace. And each time he handed out grace, he could report to me for an "attaboy" or a high-five.

As a mom, I probably did the right thing for what I knew at the time. We both needed the perspective shift and to remember the significance of grace. And it was important not to ignore his frustrations or act like they didn't have an impact. But if I could redo that stage of parenting with what I know now about creation, I think I would have made Stephen a "restoration officer."

I would have told him that his God-given sensitivity to the disorder around him was a gift to steward. He had a unique insight into things that weren't right, and he could see problems that others couldn't. His position and privilege as a child, made in the image of God, was to restore order in a way that reflected God's values and character.

Did he see someone throw a wrapper on the ground? He could pick it up because the earth is ours to steward. Did he see someone acting unkindly to another schoolmate? He could restore order by repairing the hurt classmate's heart, building her up. Did he notice a friend didn't have a snack? He could make sure to bring extras from home and share. It would be Restoration Officer to the rescue!

GENESIS

Just as Stephen voiced his frustrations about the disorder around him, we see the same things. And we don't have to wait for permission to step into the mess because God has already deemed *all* of us to be restoration officers. Let's look carefully at the roles He has assigned us and the identity we are to carry with them. Read again the Genesis verses about the creation of humanity:

> Then God said, "Let Us make man in Our image, according to Our likeness; and let them rule over the fish of the sea and

over the birds of the sky and over the cattle and over all the earth, and over every creeping thing that creeps on the earth." God created man in His own image, in the image of God He created him; male and female He created them. God blessed them; and God said to them, "Be fruitful and multiply, and fill the earth, and subdue it; and rule over the fish of the sea and over the birds of the sky and over every living thing that moves on the earth." Then God said, "Behold, I have given you every plant yielding seed that is on the surface of all the earth, and every tree which has fruit yielding seed; it shall be food for you; and to every beast of the earth and to every bird of the sky and to every thing that moves on the earth which has life, I have given every green plant for food"; and it was so. God saw all that He had made, and behold, it was very good. And there was evening and there was morning, the sixth day. (Gen. 1:26–31)

God blessed His image and gave both males and females the privilege and responsibility to be a part of His order. Verse 28 clearly lays out His threefold assignment:

1. Be fruitful and multiply.
2. Fill the earth and subdue it.
3. Rule over fish, birds, and every living thing.

Notice that the most important piece of humanity's assignment starts in verses 26 and 27. Anything we do, we are to do *as* the image of God. Therefore, as God's representatives:

1. We are to be *fruitful and multiply*, often requiring harmony and partnership.

2. We are to *fill the earth and subdue it as God's image*, not as violent authoritarians with an agenda.
3. We are to *rule as His image*, reflecting God's creativity and order.

We tend to take on the mandate but not the identity. This is something we see Adam and Eve act on in Genesis 3. Privilege without accountability is a dangerous combination. When we take on the ruling, filling, and subduing, and forget that we are representatives of a gracious and powerful God, we are in danger of using swords and spears instead of shovels and hoes (see Isa. 2:4; Mic. 4:3; and Joel 3:10).

Western Twenty-First-Century Model
Me = owner and supervisor
Others = workers

Creation Model
Yahweh = true landowner
Families (image of God) = land supervisor and land worker

It's difficult to remember the creation model when the Western twenty-first-century model pervades us. Our model has completely eliminated God, elevating ourselves to the highest position. We are accountable only to ourselves. Therefore, actively rejecting the model of our culture is difficult but necessary. Just as God challenged ANE cultures about their perception of the world, He challenges you and me.

Creation teaches us that our responsibility, first and foremost, is to God. Whatever job or role you and I have during our lifetimes, we do as His image and representative. For example, as a parent, I am accountable to God for how I raise my kids. Parenting is an incredible God-given privilege and responsibility. Of course, I'm also accountable to my kids (and spouse) for my decisions regarding their care, but that's secondary. This is across the board for every job. As a boss, apartment renter, neighbor, friend, employee, or caretaker—all of these jobs are done primarily as an image of God, not as a representative of our community or workplace or as a means to make ourselves known. We aren't given the privilege of ruling because we are so fabulous, friend. We are entrusted with His creation because He is gracious and kind and has made us able to do the job He designed for us.

It's breathtaking to know that God has given us a role in His creation and lets us act as His representative—what an incredible honor.

WORK FOR ORDER

Once we hold our identity as the image of God with humble confidence, we are ready to handle our responsibilities well.[1] In verses 28 and 29, God tells humanity to be fruitful, fill, rule, and subdue. If we aren't careful, we can use a culture-driven mindset that reads these verses as saying we have to be married with kids (fruitful and fill) and very bossy (rule and subdue). I'd like to suggest that God's command has much broader application and impact. Nuance is our friend here.

The responsibilities laid out in Genesis for men and women are related to humanity's role within the creation model. God has granted us full reign and authority over His land, giving us His permission and blessing to proceed as His representatives. It's like God set Adam and Eve in the garden, pointed to the landscape, and said, "You're just like royalty—for real! Go get it. Have fun, explore, plant, play, grow, cultivate, and steward. And do it all in the way I would do it."

I believe the ANE cultures would have heard the Genesis instructions to humanity as an expression of permission and freedom. No need to check in with an earthly king, no need to insist on hierarchies. The specific instructions (multiply, fill, rule, and subdue) were related to the role, not necessarily a checklist of items to do. Take, for example, the role of an ambassador. It's a bit like saying, "You are an ambassador; go and greet people, converse and shake hands, negotiate and strategize." Those are specific jobs related to our understanding of an ambassador. And if an ambassador doesn't do everything on the list on every occasion or even some things never at all, he is still an ambassador. Maybe his culture or environment means he needs to demonstrate flexibility in his methods. Point being, the completion of the checklist does not determine his title. In the same way, multiply, fill, rule, and subdue are descriptors of a kingly role. They aren't saying it is a job requirement to be married with kids and bossy (four-year-old me would have been very disappointed in this conclusion).

Creation paints a picture of a perfect order put together by a perfect God. This image sets up a contrast for us to hold against the disorder all around us. Working from our identity as God's image, we have an opportunity to bring restorative order to every piece of disorder we encounter, from picking up a piece of trash in the parking lot to bringing snacks to preschoolers at VBS to the UNICEF worker helping children in crisis. Whatever arena God has set you in is the place where He says: "You're responsible here—for real! Go get it. Have fun, explore, plant, play, grow, cultivate, and steward. And do it all in the way I would do it."

Genesis 1 is the model for perfect order, Genesis 3 begins the restoration process that is still ongoing even today, and Revelation 21–22 provide a sneak peek at fully restored creation. All the chapters in between give us insight into "how" this restoration happens. God is on a mission of restoration, and we are invited to participate in it alongside Him.

> **Q.** *What* is God restoring? **A.** See Genesis 1 and Revelation 21–22.
> **Q.** *How* does God restore? **A.** Genesis 3–Revelation 20.

The process of participating in restoration as God's image is a big piece of discipleship. Getting to know God and His principles and learning His "how" is why I study like crazy because I want to do it well. Doing the actual restorative work in the moment of conviction, that's the lab after the class. More times than I like to admit, I ignore the conviction or I bravely step out and my attempts at follow through fall flat.

Embracing our role as an image of God can feel vulnerable and a bit overwhelming. My best work written on my laptop doesn't always reflect what my soul wants to communicate. My attempt at parenting with an eye to restoration can end up causing frustration and irritation, resulting in tears and apologies. Our mortality infects even our finest efforts. If we aren't careful, the tension between our calling and shortcomings can keep us from trying.

Missionary, author, and theologian Lesslie Newbigin addresses this fear of failure, reminding us that our hope lies in God, not our efforts:

Our faith as Christians is that just as God raised up Jesus from the dead, so will He raise up us from the dead. And that just as all that Jesus had done in the days of His flesh seemed on Easter Saturday to be buried in final failure and oblivion, yet was by God's power raised to new life and power again, so all the faithful labor of God's servants which time seems to bury in the dust of failure, will be raised up, will be found to be there, transfigured, in the new Kingdom. Every faithful act of service, every honest labor to make the world a better place, which seemed to have been forever lost and forgotten in the rubble of history, will be seen on that day to have contributed to the perfect fellowship of God's Kingdom. As Christ, who committed Himself to God and was faithful even when all ended in utter failure and rejection, was by God raised up so that all that He had done was found to be not lost, but alive and powerful, so all who have committed their work in faithfulness to God will be by Him raised up to share in the new age, and will find that their labor was not lost, but that it has found its place in the completed Kingdom.[2]

The good news in all of this is that we are not alone. God didn't put us in our family, work, neighborhood, or city to watch us fail. He's just asking us to be faithful. If creation has taught us anything, it's that God provides, He loves to bless, and He will ultimately redeem every single action of faithfulness. This is the God we can trust when we don't know what to do, the God we can rest in because we know He reigns with grace and generosity.

COMPELLED BY COMPASSION

The story of the Good Samaritan illustrates God's restorative heart (Luke 10:25–37). Interestingly, Jesus used this story to answer a question posed to Him by a Jewish lawyer (an expert in Torah). The lawyer and Jesus had an exchange where the lawyer quoted to Jesus a mashup of a law from Deuteronomy 6:5, "You shall love the LORD your God with all your heart and with all your soul and with all your might" and one from Leviticus 19:18, "Love your neighbor as yourself." Then, the lawyer asked Jesus to define who his neighbor was, wanting to be sure he got all the details right.

Jesus told the story of the Good Samaritan in response: a man was beaten up and then left on the side of the road. Later, three men walked by him. The first two were religious Jews and did not stop. The third was a Samaritan (an ethnicity looked down upon by Jews at that time) who had compassion, stopped to help the man, and left him at a hotel with his bill paid in full. Jesus' story didn't really answer the question, "Who is my neighbor?" Instead, He described a good neighbor.

Both the lawyer and Jesus agreed that the Samaritan was the one who followed the law, treating the robbed man as a neighbor. The Samaritan saw the injured man as an image of God, one who had been beaten and left on the side of the road (disorder), and felt deep compassion for him. That compassion compelled the Samaritan to act immediately and mercifully to bring restoration.

Now, run a scenario at the grocery store. The woman in front of you with two kids sitting in the cart can't cover her bill. What do you do? First off, did you see the disorder? A woman doesn't have provision. That's not right. Secondly, compassion kicks in. This is an image of God, a woman with value and dignity, standing in a situation trying to rob her of that dignity. Beyond the recognition and the compassion, our actions may be different. Whatever we do to attempt to bring restoration will likely come from our resources, our skills, and the way God has wired us. Maybe you can:

- cover the bill
- invite her to dinner
- offer a silent prayer
- attempt to distract the rest of the line with a comedy act

I really don't know, and that's the beauty of restoration. It takes on a lot of forms and creativity.

From experience and practice in lots of labs of life, I have found that acts of restoration are often private and cost us something. They aren't putting out a political yard sign or reporting a neighbor for not mowing their lawn. Anything that starts with irritation, self-righteousness, or anger, and ends with bitterness will not lead to a restorative act on our part. Our primary motivation must be compassion and a deep longing for God's restored order.

Wiping away a child's tears, stopping by the side of the road to help someone in need, and smiling at a stressed-out cashier are all ways we can be God's image doing the work He assigned us to do. It's as simple (and difficult and heartbreaking) as recognizing order and disorder when we see it and standing in the gap.

It may be a distinction without a difference to many, but to me, grace is a part of restoration. When I made Stephen the "grace police," I was making grace the goal. If I had made him a "restoration officer," I could have helped him see that grace serves the higher purpose of restoration and that there are many paths to order.

We are all restoration officers, in a sense. And the beauty of restoration is that it has many paths. Sometimes, restoration requires justice. Sometimes, it requires grace or mercy or comfort. Study creation, study all the books between Genesis 3 and Revelation 21, and attend the lab of life ready to bless and provide—just like the God of creation has shown us how to do.

CHAPTER NINE

NO THREAT
TO THE THRONE

GENESIS 2:1–3 {DAY SEVEN}

THIS IS MY FATHER'S WORLD:
WHY SHOULD MY HEART BE SAD?
THE LORD IS KING; LET THE HEAVENS RING!
GOD REIGNS; LET THE EARTH BE GLAD!

My kids have never been able to tolerate movies with a lot of relational tension. Scratch that—*any* relational tension. When they were really little, to make it all the way through a film, I would have to dole out spoilers, "Yes, he will be okay," or "This part is rough, but it works out all right." As a preschooler, Stephen was particularly sensitive to tension. We had to leave the *Curious George* movie because the opening montage had George making all sorts of naughty choices. Stephen was so distraught, we left for a more fun activity like putt-putt.

Later, when the kids were in grade school, we entered the season of "perpetually disagreeing on what movie to watch together." (This was a long season.) As Brian and I threw out different titles and showed the kids trailers, we rarely got all three to reach a consensus. To our frustration, after each movie pitch, the kids would say, "Does it have a happy ending?" "Yes!" we would cry each time. Finally, exasperated, Brian asked them, "Have we *ever* shown you a movie with a bad ending?" and with one voice, they said, "*The Empire Strikes Back!*" I guess at least they were agreeing on something!

We all like a happy ending, and most of us are okay with a little tension or a story arc. Genesis 1–2:3 is right up my kids' alley, with a happy ending and truly no tension. It's lovely, it's creative, and nothing disrupts the flow. That wasn't the case with other ANE creation stories, though.

After God finished His work at the end of day six, He said it was very good. He made a lovely and self-perpetuating ecosystem with spoken words, gave functions to the created world, including humanity, and declared it finished. This very good and sacred world, in all of its beauty and strategic design, was ready to flourish. It truly was as good as God declared it to be.

On day seven, God rested. As we discussed in a few earlier chapters, rest is another way to say enthronement within the ANE creation genre. In seven days, a holy and sacred process was complete. Dr. John Walton aptly says, "This seventh day is not a theological appendix to the creation account, just to bring closure now that the main event of creating people has been reported. Rather, it intimates the purpose of creation and of the cosmos."[1] Everything that was laid out from the first day to the sixth defined the purpose for the earth and everything in it. Genesis 1 answered the age-old questions, "Why are we here?" and "What is our purpose?"

To ANE cultures, however, the Genesis 2:1–3 ending of the creation account feels premature. A very important piece is missing, and its absence would have flustered those around the campfire.

They would be asking, "Where's the battle? What happened to the fight scene? When does the other god come and threaten Yahweh? God is on the throne, but where are the bad guys?"

In other ANE stories, there is often a threat to the throne. The stories have a nice arc, much like many of our tales of superheroes and Jedi knights. Scholars call these elements a "cosmic battle" or "theomachy." The god in charge must defeat other gods battling for the throne or defend it. When the dust has settled, and the best god is recognized as the rightful one on the throne, *then* the story is complete.

COSMIC BATTLES

A famous battle for the throne happened in *Enuma Elish*. In this story, Marduk, the hero, has to defeat the dragon, Tiamat.

Relief drawing from the Palace of Sennacherib, commonly associated with Marduk and Tiamat from the story Epic of Creation (Enuma Elish).
Public domain.

He shot off the arrow, it broke open her belly,

It cut to her innards, it pierced the heart.

He subdued her and snuffed out her life,

He flung down her carcass, he took his stand upon it.

After the vanguard had slain Tiamat,

He scattered her forces, he dispersed her host.[2]

Now, there's a story! A hero, a bad guy, an epic battle, and a celebrated winner. Later, Marduk takes Tiamat's corpse and splits it into the sky above and land/sea below. It's gritty and gory, and my kids would have hated it, but Hollywood producers might think it has potential.

Egyptian stories were exciting too. In Egyptian understanding, creation was a daily event. Using magic, the sun god defeated a dragon (sometimes named Apep), who wanted to destroy the sun god and put the world back into chaos.[3] Creation and cosmic battles happened every evening and morning, with the sun god keeping order daily in the face of destruction.

Recalling that creation accounts are theological documents, a cosmic battle communicates that the creating god—the good god that is worshiped—is mighty and strong. He can defeat other strong gods and keep the status quo. In Genesis, our true creation account, why isn't there a battle? And what is its absence communicating to the Israelites—and to us?

BAD ASSUMPTIONS

Throughout the creative process, God has carefully removed other gods from the story, not through warfare, but with silence. By taking His throne without a cosmic battle, God is reiterating that other gods are not a part of Yahweh's reign. This was unique among all cosmogonies. No other story had a god with ultimate power—all gods face threats from other gods.

In some ways, the absence of expected features (like a cosmic battle) can land harder on the audience than simply stating what the story reveals.[4] I imagine this part was met with an odd silence at the campfire. Where was the battle? In my imagination, the grandfather telling the story leans forward and pokes the fire a bit, enjoying the confusion and waiting for the conclusions to occur to the crowd.

The absence of a battle means nothing can challenge the reign of God. As Dr. Walton says, "Unlike the other gods, he never had his authority taken from him, nor did he have to gain or regain a particular status."[5] The throne of God is not up for grabs or under any threat. They didn't have to worry about God losing power to another god (which could mean losing a war), or having a weakness to exploit.

As these fairly astounding truths about God fell on the campfire, I wonder if they were quiet or exploded in conversation. Maybe both.

The lack of a cosmic battle may surprise us too. We may have made the assumption that God and Satan are opposite powers. In our mind's eye, we have pictured it a bit like the superhero stories with good versus evil, Satan and God on an even playing field, while we keep our fingers crossed that God wins. But Genesis 1–2:3 teaches that we have no need to wonder if God will ever lose because there is no battle for God's throne.[6] There is no divine conflict. Never has been and never will be; praise God.

Other cosmogonies reflect humanity's experience with power, as their deities act much like tyrants with their power under perpetual threat. The people had seen politics get out of hand and manipulation have its way. They knew war was a very real threat, and their equilibrium was tied to the desires and actions of their kings. It made perfect sense to them that their world reflected their deities' world. The underlying methods of the gods and the people were parallel (politics, war, conspiracies, might), but the gods had an extra dose of supernatural power.

Contrast that with the description of how God carries His power. It is intrinsic to Him (no need for secret words—see chapter 4), it is without rival, and it is maintained without violence or manipulation. He is goodness itself. He blesses, provides for His creation, and delegates to humanity.

We don't really have a metric for this, do we? It's hard to conceive of a peaceful *and* tremendous power that is effortlessly good and unthreatened. The level of miraculous necessary to create a world and ecosystem out of nothing is enough to put us in awe, but the way God holds it with such stability and security makes it almost feel safe. Is that how you have pictured God? Or has your understanding of His character looked more like interactions with authority on earth?

It's tough to leave our experiences in a fallen world and let God introduce Himself anew. To let Him show us how it should be. The leadership on the global and political stage has disappointed people on all sides, and in each of our lives, we have experienced the fallout from selfish or misguided authority figures. The disappointment and pain sting. Our expectations have lowered, and our hopes might have all but disappeared, and . . .

Can I interrupt those memories and interject for a minute?

But God! He's outside those experiences and on a different level. When those feelings based on our experiences start to mirror our understanding of God, we need to take a deep breath and find a lily and a sparrow (Matt. 6:25–33). Real life is best, but pull up a video on your phone if you're desperate. Lilies and sparrows are wonderful reflections of God's character. He is powerful enough to design and make wings and petals but also caring enough to feed and clothe. That is who sits on the throne without a threat. In God's introduction to humanity, He wanted us to know who He is and how He holds power.

And it is unlike anything we have ever encountered.

UNDERMINING ORDER

There is a battle a little later in Genesis, though. When evil enters the story, it comes in the form of a serpent.[7]

> Now the serpent was more crafty than any beast of the field which the Lord God had made. And he said to the woman, "Indeed, has God said, 'You shall not eat from any tree of the garden'?" (Gen. 3:1)

Notice the serpent is identified as a wild animal "the Lord God had made." In Genesis 1:26, we see that the wild animals are under the authority of humanity. The serpent is an animal under humanity's rule; therefore, his position is already quite low.

Also, notice what the serpent attacks. He cannot go after the throne, so his play is to disrupt God's created order and undermine His word. He tempts the woman: "For God knows that in the day you eat from it your eyes will be opened, and you will be like God, knowing good and evil" (Gen. 3:5). He has her attention and is attempting to manipulate her; already he has stepped out of bounds by acting as an authority over her. But the serpent goes one step further, tempting her to mistrust and disobey God, to disrupt the order and to put herself on the throne. Dr. Averbeck states, "The challenge, and so also the battle between God and the serpent, is actually over mankind. People *are the battleground—the 'territory' under dispute*—and the central concern of this battle of the ages has as much to do with people as with the great serpent."[8]

God's Order	The Serpent's Temptation
God	Humanity and God
Humanity (image of God)	
Animals	

Creation challenges our assumption that God's authority can be thwarted. And it does this by keeping the serpent out of a battle with God. Genesis 3 notes that there is a battle—it just turns out that the serpent is a lot less powerful than he lets on. He is a created being just like anything else, and his goal is to swipe at God's creation and usurp the created order that God put into place. Satan may want to go after God,[9] but his hunting ground will be humanity and God's created order. He can't usurp God's throne. When it comes to any challenge to the created order, it happens at the earthly, human level.

There is much to say about Genesis 2 and 3, but for our purposes, know this: the serpent's activity to disrupt God's perfect order and misrepresent God's word is his only play, and he employs it repeatedly. Creation is a testimony of God's goodness and trustworthy character. If the serpent can't have the throne, he longs to bear false witness about God's character and undermine the order God put into place.

All of this is excellent news for you and me. We have no need to fear cosmic chaos with a cosmic battle underway. Day seven persists, with God seated on His throne. We know that He is not resting as a tired and uninvolved parent. Dr. Ben Witherington of Asbury Theological Seminary notes that God's "task of providential governing and intervening for his people begins when the creative task ends. He does not withdraw or take away his interests, his involvement, his governing, his relating, or his helping . . . this is critical to humanity's ongoing survival."[10] We aren't alone; the God we serve is powerful, unhindered, and deeply involved with His creation.

Day seven insists that God's hand is on the wheel. The rest of Genesis begins the story of how God patiently, slowly, and purposefully began to reorder creation after the fall.

CONSISTENT CHARACTER

When I was in high school, I drove myself to school. We lived in Minnesota, and one particular day, it snowed. The plows are excellent at clearing the snow and laying down salt or chemicals to melt the ice, so it was fairly safe for me to drive. My parents had warned me to watch for black ice, a thin layer of ice on the blacktop roads that was often difficult to see. Turning out of our neighborhood could be a little tricky, too, as people liked going fast down the crossroad. I had driven this way many times, and between the plow aid and my experience, I was pretty confident the morning would be normal.

As I made a lefthand turn out of the neighborhood and began to accelerate, I felt the wheels hit a patch of black ice, and the car started to spin. Once, then twice, I made 360-degree turns as the car spun out of control into the opposite lane and into a snowbank with a thump. My heart was racing, and tears started to form.

It had happened terribly fast. I tried to catch my breath and get my bearings, so glad that, by some miracle, no cars had been coming the opposite way during a busy time of day. I wasn't hurt, and the car seemed okay. Slowly, I pressed the accelerator and was able to inch out of the snow and onto the road carefully. I turned off the main road and back into my neighborhood, heading straight for home.

Somehow, my dad saw me coming. I have no idea how he knew I was returning home, but he was standing in the driveway in his bathrobe, watching for me. I climbed out of the car, crying, and made my way to him. "You okay?" he asked. "Yeah, I think so," I replied. After a hug and checking out the car, he told me to have a good day at school. Stunned, I just looked at him. He wanted me to drive to school? He thought I could handle it? Didn't he know I had just nearly died? (Note: I hadn't nearly died, and we both knew it, but as I have said before, I've never been nonchalant in my life and certainly wasn't at sixteen.)

I took a deep breath, and with a lot more humility, I got in the car and drove myself to school. Dad had gently and patiently restored me to driving.

Like my father, God stood there when humanity skidded out of control on sin's slippery temptation. He watched as things went from bad to awful until Genesis 12. In an act of sheer grace, God reached down and plucked a man named Abram (later Abraham) out of Ur and began to restore and reorder His creation.

How did He do it? By His word and with a blessing:

Now the LORD said to Abram,
> "Go forth from your country,
> And from your relatives
> And from your father's house,

To the land which I will show you;
And I will make you a great nation,
And I will bless you,
And make your name great;
And so you shall be a blessing;
And I will bless those who bless you,
And the one who curses you I will curse.
And in you all the families of the earth will be blessed."
(Gen. 12:1–3)

And it didn't stop with Abram. His wife, Sarai, was barren and unable to have children. God restored order, spoke His promise of a child through her, and then blessed her (Gen. 17:16). Abraham had two sons who were both blessed (Gen. 17:20; 26:3, 24). Then, Jacob insisted on a blessing and received it (Gen. 32:24–28). In Genesis, over and over, God provides for people as they face famine and threats from powerful people.

Before the fall and after the fall, God is consistently a source of goodness, provision, and blessing. His word brings order. And yet, humanity consistently insists on our own way. Like the men and women in Genesis, we want to determine what is right and wrong, ignoring God's Word or even laughing at His promises. Despite our wickedness, God displays His goodness, blesses people, and provides. And when we wonder why God doggedly chooses to bring order into our disorder, He gently leans in and points to the opening chapters of Genesis. He's restoring His creation.

The serpent is consistent, too, bringing disorder and insisting God isn't trustworthy. He undermines God's words and character at every opportunity. Our daily choice is to decide who to believe. Creation invites us to trust God, who reigns without rival, and after taking a good look at God's perfectly ordered creation, to lay down our desire to order our lives our way.

Easy peasy, right?

Just kidding. As you and I know, it's anything but easy. The only way I have found to trust God and His order, rather than myself and my order, is to do it. The long obedience in the same direction is . . . well, it's long.[11]

My grandmother, Ruth Booth, knew about long obedience. And she was a force—married twice, a mother five times over, with twenty grandchildren who adored her, thirty-two-plus great-grandchildren who were in awe of her, and a host of friends who became family. She was a nurse, a civil rights activist, a speaker, and a medical missionary.

Life threw some of its worst her way: poverty, widowhood, tuberculosis, the death of a child, widowhood a second time, and countless other personal heartbreaks. Most people would have become hardened and bitter at the winds of tragedy she faced. Instead, she remained joyful. She decided to trust God and His plans.

One of my cousins was visiting nursing homes and noticed that most people were grumpy and unhappy, but a few maintained joy. So, the next time this cousin chatted with my grandmother, my cousin asked her how she had stayed so happy. The answer? "One day at a time. One day at a time." Each day was a choice to trust. A choice for steadfast faith. And all those days added up to a lifetime of finding joy.

And through her last days, she exclaimed God's goodness, faithfulness, holiness, and tender mercy. The miracle of her life was how she allowed God to turn her passion for justice into acts of amazing mercy and bravery. She was highly attuned to the hardships others faced and became an advocate for those who didn't have one. On one occasion, she and my PawPaw drove *toward* a chemical explosion to help people. Another time, she sat on a bus, choosing a seat between a man and the woman he was berating. He turned his anger on my grandmother—exactly her intent. She told me, "That poor girl couldn't say anything back to that man. But I could take a little heat off her for a bit."

She had a marriage that was the definition of faithfulness, and she died peacefully the day before what would have been their seventy-third wedding anniversary. The romantic in me thinks PawPaw had a bouquet of purple flowers ready for her. Even more important, though, was her relationship with God. She loved Him with a tenacity that belied her small physical frame. Every conversation with her would somehow include an example of something she learned from an interaction with Him, and undoubtedly, she would testify to the value of trusting God.

Her circumstances never dictated her worshipful posture toward God. Some think it's a weak person who chooses to yield to God in all things—especially in the face of unimaginable sorrow. I think it made her a force.

We choose who we truly believe is in charge one day at a time. And as someone who has tried to live this, I can say that the choice *does* get easier if we are consistent. God's faithfulness becomes more palpable, His consistent character less something others talk about and more of a reality. I saw my grandmother choose, but more than that, I can see God's faithfulness in my own life. I not only point to her story, but to my own, each and every foggy day seven with God on the throne.

CHAPTER TEN

SABBATH FOR RESTLESS HEARTS

THIS IS MY FATHER'S WORLD,
HE SHINES IN ALL THAT'S FAIR;
IN THE RUSTLING GRASS I HEAR HIM PASS;
HE SPEAKS TO ME EVERYWHERE.

For most of my life, Sabbath involved church in the morning, grocery shopping for the week on the way home, and—depending on the season—football on TV, reading by a fire, or walks through the neighborhood. Sundays had a slow and steady rhythm, a way to prepare for the week and a way to slow down the pace just enough to catch our breath.

When Clara was sick, I stopped planning for anything except doctor visits. Every day depended on how the chemo interacted with an ill six-year-old, so we woke up and let the day happen. What are we having for dinner? I didn't know. Could we join friends at the park? Not a clue. Did the kids have any school events coming up? I couldn't tell you. If I tried to put any of those things on our calendar, it was an exercise in frustration, resulting in canceled plans and disappointed kids. We could not make choices that had been at our fingertips just a few short months earlier.

It was exhausting living under the tyrant of disease. Cancer was the variable with the final say. For Brian and me, the weight was ever-present. For Abbie and Stephen, the uncertainty of not knowing who would greet them as they came home from school was unsettling. And dear Clara could only focus on keeping food down and pain under control.

An odd hopelessness falls on a home that can't make plans. Our options were dictated by destructive cancer cells and their poisonous cure. The only option was to wait out the season and fix our eyes on the future for a day when Clara would be well and we could return to normal. Every day was hard. And we knew the weeks ahead would be rough. And the months weren't looking any better. But next year? We hoped it would be different. We dreamed of heading out to visit friends when we wanted to. We longed to return to making our favorite meals and taking vacations, and Mom being home to meet the school bus every day.

Every night, when I laid my head on my pillow, I felt pure relief we had made it through that day. Somehow, the exhaustion of the day and the impossibility of making plans forced me to give up trying to know all the answers beforehand or fill the slots in my calendar. The sun had risen and set, we had full bellies, and the kids knew they were loved and safe. If I overthought about the next day, I couldn't sleep; I just had to sigh and know it was coming. As I closed my eyes, I prayed that the same mercies that got me through that day would meet me in the morning.

During that season, the habits that had guided our Sunday routine were hit or miss, and honestly, when we had a "normal" Sunday, it still didn't provide reprieve. Why didn't it help? What was I doing wrong?

I needed more than a Sabbath break from the daily grind. I needed a Sabbath from cancer.

SABBATH ORIGINS

Genesis

On the seventh day of creation, as the climax of the story, God rested. In Hebrew, the root word is *šabāt* (pronounced sha-VAT), from which we get Sabbath, the day of rest. As we've discussed, rest was sitting on the throne, establishing God's reign. It signified to the ancient reader that creation was complete and ready to roll.

Manna and Quail

After creation, the Sabbath disappears from the biblical narrative until the next book in the Bible, Exodus. After God led the Israelites out of Egypt and saved them from slavery, they were on a long journey to a promised land that God would let them have as their own. On their travels, they became hungry and grumbled against their leaders, Moses and Aaron, saying they had certainly eaten better in Egypt and feared they would starve in the desert.

God gave Moses precise instructions for the people in Exodus 16, which probably seemed quite strange. Every morning, God provided bread (manna), and every evening He provided meat (quail). Everyone gathered what they needed that day but could not keep extra for the next day. Some Israelites tried to keep it overnight anyway, just in case (confession: I totally would have been that kind of Israelite) and found it rotten the next day.

The manna and quail were a miraculous provision, but I wonder if there was an element of stress every evening when the Israelites went to bed. What if God didn't provide the following day? What if they sinned and God pulled the resources of quail and manna? Going to bed every evening with an empty pantry would have to be an act of forced faith. After all, in the desert, miraculous manna and quail were the only culinary options. It's a little like waking up every morning to a bank account with only enough for that day and seeing a balance of zero every evening.

If you've ever lived hand to mouth, paycheck to paycheck, unsure about where your following resources will come from, you understand this stress deeply. There's an undercurrent of discomfort and unease that feels like a pot at a perpetual simmer, ready to boil over at any moment. Tomorrow is another day of survival, and the next day will be the same. The cycle can feel unbreakable and hopeless.

For Israel, living with forced faith and gathering only enough for a day at a time was reprieved on the sixth day:

> "See, the Lord has given you the sabbath; therefore He gives you bread for two days on the sixth day. Remain every man in his place; let no man go out of his place on the seventh day." So the people rested on the seventh day. (Ex. 16:29–30)

On the sixth day, Israel was invited to gather and keep enough in their pantry for the following day. One night a week, they went to bed, pantry full. As a gift, they had tomorrow's provision lining their cupboards. As a gift, the next day, they would eat without having to gather it from the ground. On the seventh day, they woke up to a full pantry, enough for the day.

The seventh day was "a sabbath observance, a holy sabbath to the Lord" (Ex. 16:23). "So the people rested on the seventh day" (Ex. 16:30). And as they rested on that holy Sabbath to the Lord, they were physically reminded that the God of creation had a good order and desire to provide for His people. God's character to provide for their physical needs of food and rest was on display in this Sabbath celebration.

The entire week was a repeatable pattern. The people worked for six days, gathering what God had provided, and on the seventh day, they rested in the double provision from the day before. God's reign over His good order, demonstrating His good character to provide in abundance for His people, was put into a very practical 6:1 lived-out rhythm.

Do you think the Israelites eventually understood the nature of God to provide? Perhaps after a few years, they woke up expecting manna and quail, enough to get their daily nutrition and sustenance. Did they know God's pantry was full, which meant theirs was also? As their children grew, did they tell them about God's goodness to bring them out of slavery and give them what they needed daily? Did they point out that God made the birds and could direct them? Every dawn, as they ate of God's new mercies, did they marvel that God created the ground, clouds, and ecosystem that were designed to flourish?

What a beautiful thing it would be if the Israelites' forced faith relaxed into relieved faith, if their hopelessness shifted to peace. There wasn't a blasted thing that the Israelites could do to provide for themselves in the desert. But they could loosen clenched fists, finding joy and peace, knowing that God would have it covered seven days a week and only asked them to gather six days.

God said the Sabbath was a gift *for* Israel *from* God (Ex. 16:29). On the seventh day, when they stayed in their tents, they rested to honor His provision and request. God, the Creator of the universe and the One who saved them, saw the value in a 6:1 rhythm of work and rest, stewarding every day and the holy day.

The Ten Commandments

Three short chapters after the miracle of manna and quail (that the Israelites were still eating every day), God invited the people of Israel to be in a covenant relationship with Him. If they agreed to follow His values and principles, God would make them His treasured possession, and they would be a kingdom of His priests (Ex. 19:5–6). God laid out ten commandments for the people (followed by many more principles and standards), including a specific command about the Sabbath:

> "Remember the sabbath day, to keep it holy. Six days you shall labor and do all your work, but the seventh day is a sabbath of the LORD your God; in it you shall not do any work, you or your son or your daughter, your male or your female servant or your cattle or your sojourner who stays with you. For in six days the LORD made the heavens and the earth, the sea and all that is in them, and rested on the seventh day; therefore the LORD blessed the sabbath day and made it holy." (Ex. 20:8–11)

The Israelites were already in a pattern of labor for six days and rest on the seventh, and in this command, the Lord ties the pattern to creation. He sat down to reign on the seventh day; we stop our work to honor His reign (not to mimic it). The day is blessed and holy and still exists as a gift for humanity. To stop, find relaxed faith in God's provision, and remember the character of the One who reigns over it all—that is a gift.

REST FOR OUR MINDS AND SOULS

The Exodus instructions about the Sabbath insist that work stops, perhaps because we have an undercurrent of anxiety that we don't quite have enough. Provision is one of those things that's hard to unclench our fists around. In this broken world, where the weeds fight to choke out fruitful crops, it's not a surprise that we feel our provision is desperate and up to us. We tend to lead with a sense of lack, an unquenchable desire to get just a little more in our stockpile and ensure we're covered for the near and far future.

When Abbie was a toddler, she loved pacifiers. She and Clara both used them (they were eleven months apart), so we had plenty around the house. Every evening, when I checked on Abbie before heading to bed, I'd find at least five or six pacifiers in her crib. Somehow, she managed to find as many pacifiers as she could during the day and stockpiled them. As I peeked in the room she shared with Clara, I often saw two or three set like a little halo around her head as she slept on her back, arms outstretched with each hand cradling a pacifier and her mouth loosely holding one.

It's challenging to sleep, not knowing if we will have what we need the next day. We stockpile in our storehouses of banks and kitchen pantries, but those things are less trustworthy than we think. A natural disaster, pandemic, economic crisis, war, or irresponsible behavior of someone outside our control can wipe us out without warning. And funny enough, our response to this truth is to diversify our stockpiles to outsmart the system. Like Abbie, we keep adding to our stash.

Once a week, God says: stop.

Sabbath forces us to look our self-sufficiency in the eyeballs and insist it yield to a more trustworthy provider than ourselves. On Sabbath, we remember that we can't outrun disaster or guarantee health, that our accumulation is not a failsafe, and we slowly unclench our fists and relax into confidence that our trustworthy God is on the throne.

It's not enough to only stop our bodies. For us to honor God's reign with a nap and a promise not to open our laptops, yet still proceed to fret about our kids/work/relationships/money is disobeying the commandment in our hearts. Our bodies *and* our souls need the rest provided in the 6:1 rhythm.

The gift of the Sabbath is not found in just stopping. That's nice, but the act of stopping is neutral at best. The gift is when we reorientate ourselves toward God, rededicate our trust, and meditate on His trustworthiness. If we stop and focus on the ceasing, we chase rules or check boxes and call it "success." Like my experience trying to continue the habits that had guided our Sunday routine before cancer invaded our home, we did the right things but didn't find rest. When I stopped on Sundays to catch a breath and get ready for the week, I was trying to keep the Sabbath by mimicking God. Unfortunately, that meant I was setting up *my* kingdom for *my* week, resting in preparation to run *my* show.

To honor God's reign when I rest and prepare for the coming week, I need to remember my dependence and God's goodness. I have to stop and look at the sacred map in Genesis 1–2:3, the creation He designed to flourish, and intentionally reorient toward His character. The problems I face I can take directly to Him. I examine any fears that are disguising a god that snuck into my pantheon. And I humbly ask God to open my calendar and my heart to any place He would allow me to act as a part of His restorative plan.

When the Israelites stopped gathering manna once a week, I bet their children asked why. The "why" carries the Sabbath focus. And with every answer that every mom or dad gave their kids, they declared that God was trustworthy and good and that He provided.

When our bodies stop working and minds stop worrying,

to Sabbath is to fill the void with our "why." And that is where we find the gift of Sabbath—honoring God's reign and relaxing into trust.

SABBATH FAILS

Prophets

After God gave Israel the Ten Commandments, the nation grew for six hundred years, established a kingship, split into two kingdoms (Israel to the north and Judah to the south), and made themselves a part of the political landscape in the region. Neither kingdom did a stellar job of keeping the principles and commands God had given the people as they traveled through the wilderness. God sent prophets to warn them that they were steering danger-ously off course.

The prophet Isaiah spoke to the southern kingdom of Judah, calling attention to the futility of participating in religious activity but ignoring the principles God cares about:

"Bring your worthless offerings no longer,
Incense is an abomination to Me.
New moon and sabbath, the calling of assemblies—
I cannot endure iniquity and the solemn assembly.
"I hate your new moon festivals and your appointed feasts,
They have become a burden to Me;
I am weary of bearing them.
"So when you spread out your hands in prayer,
I will hide My eyes from you;
Yes, even though you multiply prayers,
I will not listen.
Your hands are covered with blood.

"Wash yourselves, make yourselves clean;
Remove the evil of your deeds from My sight.
Cease to do evil,
Learn to do good;
Seek justice,
Reprove the ruthless,
Defend the orphan,
Plead for the widow." (Isa. 1:13–17)

God told His people they were participating in the Sabbath activities and rules but completely neglecting His values and principles the other six days of the week. His reign was not reflected in their daily walk, only in their weekly performance. The hands they raised in praise were covered in the blood of people they hurt.

They walked by the vulnerable and hurting, shrugging at injustice, ignoring the oppressed Sunday through Friday. Then, on Saturday, they declared that God reigned and that they had the honor and responsibility of representing His values (listed in Isaiah: do right, seek justice, defend the oppressed, aid the vulnerable). God finds that mindset a burden, wearisome, and unbearable.

Around the same time, the prophet Amos spoke to the people of the northern kingdom, warning them their economic security had made them unconcerned for the poor (Amos 2:7; 5:11) and condemned their sketchy business practices (Amos 5:6–7, 12). Just as God told the people of Judah, He said to those in Israel that their actions during the week did not match the meaning of celebrating the Sabbath, so He did not accept their practice of festivals and Sabbath (Amos 5:21–26).

Hear this, you who trample the needy, to do away with the humble of the land, saying,

> "When will the new moon be over,
> So that we may sell grain,
> And the sabbath, that we may open the wheat market,
> To make the bushel smaller and the shekel bigger,
> And to cheat with dishonest scales,
> So as to buy the helpless for money
> And the needy for a pair of sandals,
> And that we may sell the refuse of the wheat?"
> (Amos 8:4–6)

Can you hear God's frustration? Instead of recognizing the reign of God, their provider and sustainer, they saw the Sabbath as a profit loss, messing with their margins. Their perspective was all out of whack, and their Sunday to Friday was telling on them.

It wasn't that they were irreligious from Sunday to Friday. God points out that their system of worship six days a week centered on their government, idols, and gold. Then, on the Sabbath, they tried to pull a switcheroo and put God on the throne. They were worshiping their kingdoms, not God's. But it didn't work for them, and it doesn't work for us. God will not be mocked and let us represent Him halfway.

The week's rhythm is 6:1, which had become a solitary drumbeat, but the one won't ever work without the six. Following the steps of the Sabbath without participating in God's restorative and redemptive vision the rest of the week . . . well, God said it stinks.

Sabbath Meals

Fifteen hundred years later, when Jesus walked Israel, the Sabbath had quite a few rules around it.[1] These additional laws were meant as a sort of guardrail to help the Jewish people keep the Sabbath. As the religious teachers of the day saw Jesus breaking some of the extra laws (that weren't in the Old Testament), they were alarmed. Their concern was not entirely about the law itself but the slippery slope that might be just on the other side of breaking Sabbath restrictions.

On one specific Sabbath, the Pharisees (influential religious teachers of the day[2]) were waiting and watching to see if Jesus would break the Sabbath rules.

> One Sabbath day as Jesus was walking through some grainfields, his disciples began breaking off heads of grain to eat. But the Pharisees said to Jesus, "Look, why are they breaking the law by harvesting grain on the Sabbath?"
>
> Jesus said to them, "Haven't you ever read in the Scriptures what David did when he and his companions were hungry? He went into the house of God (during the days when Abiathar was high priest) and broke the law by eating the sacred loaves of bread that only the priests are allowed to eat. He also gave some to his companions."
>
> Then Jesus said to them, "The Sabbath was made to meet the needs of people, and not people to meet the requirements of the Sabbath. So the Son of Man is Lord, even over the Sabbath!" (Mark 2:23–28 NLT)

While the Pharisees were focused on the dangers of slippery slopes, they missed the goal of the Sabbath. Jesus responded by reminding them that God's rules are designed to reinforce principles; rules aren't meant to support rules.[3]

I wonder if Jesus' allusion to Exodus 16:29 ("See, the LORD has given you the sabbath") was meant to bring the conversation back to the intention of the Sabbath that the Pharisees had forgotten. In essence, the devout were serving the Sabbath rules, not letting the Sabbath provide a rhythm for work and a reminder of their provision's source.

The laws surrounding the Sabbath observance had flipped the emphasis so that man was indeed serving the Sabbath, bowing down to the rules rather than letting the day of rest remind them of their abundant provision. They were counting how many steps were considered "work" rather than counting the ways God had provided for them.

Rules That Keep Us Restless

Israel missed the Sabbath for the rules both pre-exile and post-exile. The prophets spoke to those in Israel who were treating the Sabbath like a checkbox so they could get on with their lives. It was an interruption at best and a total inconvenience at worst. They were practicing the Sabbath (and other religious festivals) to appease God and get back to living the lives they wanted.

After the exile, the Pharisees focused on Sabbath rules because they wanted to get it right. As they recalled the exile and the dismissive attitude of the Israelites, they tried to ensure people didn't fall away again, so they developed additional rules to help people know what to do. Somehow, a strict adherence to the rhythm superseded the principles that were the foundation for the rhythm. Sabbath became an obligation, a way to appease God and to ensure a right relationship with Him.

It's important to remember that compared to other Jewish religious groups, the Pharisees of the day were influential but considered too lenient by some sects.[4] Truly, they just wanted to adhere to the Old Testament covenant as best as possible. Sometimes, we fall into the trap of rolling our eyes at "those Pharisees," forgetting they can serve as a mirror for our own misapplied best efforts at obedience.

Whether we want to check off the Sabbath box in order to go about our week, or if we like guardrails to keep us safely in the Sabbath green zone, both rule-focused orientations miss that the Sabbath is a gift.

The Pharisees focused on what we shouldn't do, but stopping was supposed to push us to see what God does. It's inconceivable that the men following God across farmland, with kernels formed from seeds God Himself created, would not be allowed the sustenance of that grain. As Jesus brought the kingdom of God to earth, with God's values and principles, it would be the most natural thing in the world for the disciples to reach down and pluck from a prepared pantry filled with grain.

The rhythm of a work week is important and helpful. For six days, we work in tandem with God's abundant provision. On those six days, we strive and work with the bodies He gave us, breathing the air He provided. And one day we don't work. We pause and remember, we pause and give thanks, we pause and reflect on the character of a God who delights to give good things. If we're afraid of the Sabbath—worried that we may work too much and make God angry, fearful that eating a piece of grain will create displeasure and it's better to go hungry—well, we've truly missed it.

God is a provider. The way He designed the world to function and flourish, His invitation to work in an ecosystem that thrives, and His invitation to the rhythm of 6:1 reiterate that we can trust God to provide enough. Jesus invites us to walk alongside Him, the one who was with God in the beginning, and reach down and feel the grains at our fingertips when our stomachs growl. He is trustworthy to provide.

SABBATH RESTORATION

Jesus' most contested interactions with the Pharisees about the Sabbath revolved around healing. Jesus did seven recorded healings on the Sabbath.[5] The book of Mark describes Jesus deliberately bringing the issue of the Sabbath and healing to the center:

> Jesus went into the synagogue again and noticed a man with a deformed hand. Since it was the Sabbath, Jesus' enemies watched him closely. If he healed the man's hand, they planned to accuse him of working on the Sabbath.
>
> Jesus said to the man with the deformed hand, "Come and stand in front of everyone." Then he turned to his critics and asked, "Does the law permit good deeds on the Sabbath, or is it a day for doing evil? Is this a day to save life or to destroy it?" But they wouldn't answer him.
>
> He looked around at them angrily and was deeply saddened by their hard hearts. Then he said to the man, "Hold out your hand." So the man held out his hand, and it was restored! At once the Pharisees went away and met with the supporters of Herod to plot how to kill Jesus. (Mark 3:1–6 NLT)

The Pharisees knew good and well that it was lawful to save a life on the Sabbath but refused to say so and give Jesus the upper hand. They had fallen into the trap of wanting to win an argument rather than engage in a discussion where their minds might be changed. Indeed, they had already made their minds up about Jesus, and in their estimation, He was dangerous. He was pulling the people down that slippery slope and needed to be stopped. In their stubbornness, though, they missed hearing Jesus' lesson about the Sabbath and His ministry.

Try to picture the crowded room from Mark's narrative, people peeking over each other to see what was happening. Jesus, who was with God in the beginning and created humankind, called up a man with a shriveled hand. Imagine the hush as Jesus asked a very pointed question: "Does the law permit good deeds on the Sabbath, or is it a day for doing evil? Is this a day to save life or to destroy it?" (Mark 3:4). See Jesus' face as He becomes distressed and angry that the room could not answer His question.

I feel Jesus was distressed because they did not know the nature of God. The people were so confused about the law, bogged down by guardrails, and disoriented by their political situation that they could not step through the fog and say, "Yes! Of course, it's right to heal him even on the Sabbath!" From creation, God demonstrated His delight in making good things, setting them free to flourish and grow, giving men and women the authority to govern under His good reign. He commanded with a word, demonstrated power without violence, and created beauty without defect. And, as He stood beside one of His created beings with a shriveled hand, the people didn't know if God would want him healed because it was Saturday.

It would make me sad if my kids misunderstood my character. Nothing makes me happier than when my kids offer our home to friends without first asking. If they have a friend who is hungry or lonely or having a tough time at their house, it brings great joy to my heart when they say, "You can come to stay with us. I know it's okay. I don't have to ask." If the kids were more worried about having the house clean or a nice meal prepared than alleviating a tough spot for their friends, I would be distressed indeed. Yes, we usually clean before people come over. And yeah, I typically plan out our meals. But in the face of someone who needs help, all those things are unimportant.

God stood beside a man with a shriveled hand and said to the crowd, "Don't you even know? Of course, I will heal him." The religious teachers of the day would leave the man to suffer for the sake of a holy day. Jesus would heal because He was bringing His holy kingdom to earth. In its most concentrated form, the kingdom of God is a complete restoration of creation with God among us. Part of Jesus' sneak peek into a fully restored creation was His healing and raising the dead—a picture of holiness spreading outward from His very body, overpowering the effects of brokenness. As the Sabbath celebrates God's reign, wonders at His lovely order, and remembers His nature to provide, Jesus' healing a shriveled hand was wonderfully in line with bringing the kingdom to earth.

After healing a blind man, when the Pharisees were questioning Jesus, He said, "My Father is working until now, and I Myself am working" (John 5:17b). In a sense, Jesus was saying, "I'm doing My job. This is who I am."

Even as Jesus violated Israel's Sabbath rules, He demonstrated the principles of the Sabbath. When He placed their rule next to His principle and asked them to make a choice, the Jews of Jesus' day were so confounded. They looked at a man with a shriveled hand and did not know if it was the right thing to heal him. How terrifying to stand at the guardrail, well-meaning and concerned, and discover you are on the wrong road entirely.

Oh, I pray God saves me from my errant guardrails. I typically don't recognize them until I get to the spot where I would rather others sit in their pain than have my guardrail endure a painful crash. But when Jesus presents me with a choice—restoration or rules—I pray I can't help but fall on my knees with gratitude that God is more gracious than I am. I hope to have the courage to choose restoration for myself and others every time.

KINGDOM SHOW-AND-TELL

When Jesus healed the sick and was not bothered when His disciples picked grain to eat on the Sabbath, He brought the kingdom to earth. With every action and teaching, He strategically demonstrated what His kingdom looked like. The people of Israel were thinking about a political kingdom (like that of King David), but Jesus washed feet, forgave, healed, prayed, and fed. . . . Jesus *did* God's kingdom. Healing on the Sabbath was an intentional part of His kingdom's teaching. From His first breath on earth until His death, Jesus did kingdom show-and-tell. That was His good news—the kingdom is here!

And with His resurrection, He inaugurated that kingdom. He was the first to rise, initiating the restoration promised to us and His creation.

During Sabbath, we recognize that we dwell in the *already* of God's inaugurated kingdom and the *not yet* fully restored creation. We are thankful for the already and hopeful for the not yet, peering through the foggy day-seven reality and trusting that the restoration is coming. When we take a day to remember God's holy plan, His boundless goodness, and His longing to restore, we will find the gift of trust in His reign.

We still like to make Sabbath about rules, even as we insist that we aren't. A slow scroll through current publications about the Sabbath will give oodles of ideas for guardrails and places that we should "stop." It's natural to want clear guidelines. Black and white are clear and distinct; we can differentiate with little effort. But Sabbath puts people who like rules in a bind because God doesn't give us many Sabbath rules; He focuses on what Sabbath is about. Aligning with principles requires wisdom and understanding, nuance and work, and more time and patience than many of us want to spend.

It's a little like when the expert in Jewish law cited, "love your neighbor as yourself" and then asked Jesus, "Who is my neighbor?" (Luke 10:29–37). He wanted Jesus to define it so he could make sure he was following the "loving" rules, but Jesus responded with a parable that had an even harder principle to follow. Jesus answered "Who is my neighbor?" with a description of a good neighbor (one who had compassion and acted on it), in a way saying that they were focused on the wrong question.

When the religious leaders suggested that picking wheat was against the Sabbath, Jesus said they missed the principle. When the crowds didn't know if it was right to heal on the Sabbath, Jesus was distressed at their confusion and healed the man. The focus on the Sabbath had become rules; when they asked, "Is it okay to do this on the Sabbath?" they missed the gift of trusting and knowing God.

When we say, "What do we stop?" or "What do we do?" we're looking for easy answers that will never push us to get to know and trust God. The rules in themselves will leave us feeling self-righteous and distant from God. A better question to ask ourselves might be, "Where am I struggling to trust God?" Forcing our faith and stopping our attempt to sandbag that area once a week—maybe that's a Sabbath for you. If there are places in life you can "stop" striving for control, that simple act of humble self-discipline might be your Sabbath.

What would trusting God fully with your family's well-being or your marriage look like? How about your health? What about finances and employment? Or the unforgiveness that has shifted to bitterness? We all have spots that are particularly sensitive—it's probably the one that made you a little defensive when you read it. I've still got quite a few I'm working through too.

I don't know about you, but I know for sure I've gotten to the point of full trust when I don't want to take back control. It took me years, but I got to that place with my kids. It doesn't mean I don't have concerns, or frustrations, or spend time on my knees in prayer for them. It *does* mean that I start and leave every inter-action with God glad that He has them. I feel they are in better hands with Him than with me; it's become a foundational truth I fully lean on. I'm thankful that a trustworthy God has it covered.

To be brutally honest, though, those spots of full trust aren't as many as I'd like. I have many areas of forced faith, with some shifting to relaxed faith, and precious few are full trust. But I'm getting there, one Sabbath rest in His reign at a time.

As I've shifted (slower than I want to admit) from a forced faith to a relaxed faith over the things I've been most anxious about losing control of, I realized that many times I was short-sighted. When I remember the time cancer ruled the equilibrium in my home, my greatest desire was to see my home restored to what it used to be. My dreams involved resumed play dates, normal daily routines, and sustained peace with an occasional hiccup. The goal was relief and reprieve, and above all, a healed kid. Was it wrong to want that kind of restoration? I don't think so. But I was missing God's desire for complete healing if I was fully satisfied by patches and Band-Aids.

I wish I had known enough then to have taken Sabbath to meditate on God's desire to heal *all* cancer, not just my kid's cancer. If I had the awareness and knowledge to sit in God's character, His creative bent, and remembered the reign that oversees it all, I may have enjoyed a double portion of mercy on that day.

God was ever-present in every bit of our family's suffering, and in His mercy, He *did* restore all those things to us in one way or another, but I'm so thankful that the plan doesn't end there. God looks to creation for the restoration plan, not my relief and reprieve. He aims to restore bodies so that cells don't multiply without a purpose, ultimately destroying what's in their place. He's after completely healed relationships that work in cooperation. He will eliminate obstacles to thriving. God's character is to want that for you and me because we are His creation in His world.

Someday, we will all be healed from our diseases; we will walk in God's presence and reach down for a bite to eat. Gentle Jesus will quiet our restless hearts. The fog of living marked by brokenness will lift, clarity will fall, and the not-yet-fully restored creation will be realized.

Until then, we rest in His reign, trusting Him more and more.

And in that I rest assured.

DISCUSSION QUESTIONS

CHAPTER 1

1. Have you thought about the way an ancient Israelite would have understood creation? What kind of things do you think they were concerned with?

2. When have you felt the most restful in your relationships with others and God?

3. Do you have any exposure to the creation debate in Christian evangelical circles? Do you agree that those issues don't belong in the Genesis room? Why or why not?

4. What part of this chapter has been the most challenging, uncomfortable, or confusing? Why?

CHAPTER 2

1. Read Genesis 26:1–11 and Psalm 105:1–15.
   - What do these two Scripture passages have in common with each other?
   - How do these two passages differ from each other?

2. Did you find yourself more concerned with *how* or *why* creation happened? How has looking at the questions of purpose shifted your understanding?

3. Why does knowing the style of literature in a biblical book you are reading matter?

4. What are some reasons you've learned it's important to read creation as ancient cosmogony? In your own words, how would you describe a cosmogony?

CHAPTER 3

1. How would you define *sacred*? Has that changed after reading this chapter? Why or why not?

2. Have you ever thought of creation as theology? How does approaching it as theology change the way you view it?

3. Which day of creation are you most excited to learn more about? Why?

4. Creation as a set stage for the rest of the Bible may be a new idea to you. What are ways that you can incorporate creation into the way you read the rest of the Bible?

CHAPTER 4

1. How do the ancient cosmogonies from Egypt and Babylon strike you? Do you like reading them? How have they changed the way you read Genesis?

2. Have you ever thought about Genesis 1:1–3 as describing chaos? If not, how did you think of it before? How has this chapter changed your view of the opening lines of Genesis?

3. Does it surprise you that all ANE gods are gods of order? Why or why not?

4. Have you ever been tempted to pray a specific prayer, hoping that special words could unleash God's power in your life? If so, why?

5. Has this chapter changed how you will approach God? If so, how?

CHAPTER 5

1. Have you encountered a chart that detailed the organization of God's creation (habitats/inhabitants) before? How did it strike you?

2. Have you ever thought about why God called creation "good"? In what ways does knowing that creation reflects God's goodness impact your view of God?

3. For me, predictable thriving would be sitting down and writing without struggle, knowing the exact right parenting or marriage move, or the meals I make always coming out delicious. What would predictable thriving look like in your environment?

4. Do you agree that our frustration at the present state of the world is appropriate? Does it give you hope to know it's not supposed to be this way? Why or why not?

5. What do you think about "living in the dissonance"? What areas of life feel particularly discordant right now?

CHAPTER 6

1. Names were a big deal in the ANE. Are names a big deal to you? What are some creative names you've had for items?

2. The ancient person thoughtfully and theologically integrated nature into their religion. How does learning this change how you read the creation story?

3. Looking back at the chart of Genesis 1:14–18, if you were taught the biblical account of creation as a child, which side of the chart were you taught? How would you teach the right side of the chart to a ten-year-old?

4. Had you ever noticed that the sun and moon aren't named in creation? How did it strike you when you found out that God was intentional about not naming them? Why?

5. Take a minute and think about when/where/how you've had your biggest fear or anger over the last month. Recalling those feelings and events, see if you can fill out the chart below. I've started it with examples from the book. How do your findings impact you?

Action	Fear	What I'm Serving
Overly controlling of diet or cleanliness	Disease	My health
Tightfisted	Losing my savings	Self-sufficiency

CHAPTER 7

1. What would your family portrait look like? What items would be in your picture?

2. Compare the ANE household model and the creation model. What stands out to you? What do you think a twenty-first-century model would look like?

3. Have you felt as if you needed to provide for God? If so, in what ways?

4. How have you thought of your work—as important or unimportant? Has this chapter changed your understanding of your work? How?

5. What do you think about the statement: "Any success I have is an outpouring of God's provision combined with my best efforts at stewardship; it's a dual effort"? Do you agree or disagree? Why?

CHAPTER 8

1. What do you think of humanity's threefold assignment? How does adding "as an image of God" to each of those assignments change your understanding? How does adding "as an image of God" to your responsibilities (dishwasher, employee, parent, friend, etc.) challenge you?

2. What areas in your life (family, friends, work, neighborhood, church, government, etc.) are the most difficult to remember that you are accountable to God for the manner in which you work? Why?

3. Read this quote by Lesslie Newbigin aloud:

Our faith as Christians is that just as God raised up Jesus from the dead, so will He raise up us from the dead. And that just as all that Jesus had done in the days of His flesh seemed on Easter Saturday to be buried in final failure and oblivion, yet was by God's power raised to new life and power again, so all the faithful labor of God's servants which time seems to bury in the dust of failure, will be raised up, will be found to be there, transfigured, in the new Kingdom. Every faithful act of service, every honest labor to make the world a better place, which seemed to have been forever lost and forgotten in the rubble of history, will be seen on that day to have contributed to the perfect fellowship of God's Kingdom. As Christ, who committed Himself to God and was faithful even when all ended in utter failure and rejection, was by God raised up so that all that He had done was found to be not lost, but alive and powerful, so all who have committed their work in faithfulness to God will be by Him raised up to share in the new age, and will find that their labor was not lost, but that it has found its place in the completed Kingdom.[1]

Have you ever thought about God resurrecting efforts and work that are done in faithfulness? How does that thought encourage you to persevere?

4. The parable of the good Samaritan encourages us to be a good neighbor. How are you challenged and encouraged by Jesus' story?

5. What are ways you encounter disorder in your daily life? I used an example at a grocery store. Can you think of a similar one?

CHAPTER 9

1. The absence of a cosmic battle in Genesis 1 would have baffled the ANE individual, but you and I have likely never wondered about it. How does knowing God does not have a threat to the throne impact your understanding of Him?

2. When there is a battle, it occurs at the level of humanity. Look at the temptation the serpent spoke to Eve. We've all been tempted to put ourselves on equal footing with God by insisting that we can determine right and wrong, not God. In what ways can we combat this temptation? In what areas of your life do you want to decide what is right and wrong?

3. After Genesis 3, the serpent disappears from the story. Why do you think that is?

4. God patiently starts the restoration plan beginning in Genesis 12. If you're familiar with any stories in Genesis, discuss ways God offered blessings to individuals and families.

CHAPTER 10

1. What did "Sabbath" look like in your home growing up? How has that shaped your view of God's character?

2. The Sabbath origins (creation, manna and quail, and the Ten Commandments) can sometimes feel disjointed. In what ways do they all describe God's reign? (See also the preamble to the Ten Commandments in Exodus 20:2.)

3. Treating the Sabbath like an obligation so we can get on with our lives (as pre-exile Israel was) or as a checkbox for religious piety (as the Pharisees were) are both missing the principle of the Sabbath. How would you define the Sabbath principle? Do you tend to fall in the "obligation" or "checkbox" category?

4. Read Mark 3:1–6 aloud. Try to picture the scene and how it impacted the crowd, the Pharisees, and the man who was healed. Where do you think you would be in the scene?

5. How can we practically stop and recognize God's reign without getting caught in the "obligation" or "checkbox" ditches?

FURTHER RESOURCES

(Linked at rachelboothsmith.com/rest-assured)

CHAPTER 1

READ
- *How to Read the Bible for All It's Worth: A Guide to Understanding the Bible* by Gordon D. Fee and Douglas Stuart

LISTEN
- *Pillar Podcast*, "Hitching the Old Testament to the New. Part 4: Creation," June 25, 2018 (32 min)
- "Restless" by Audrey Assad on her 2010 album *The House You're Building* (5 min)
- "He's Always Been Faithful" by Sara Groves on her 2001 album *Conversations* (3.5 min)

WATCH
- Dr. John Walton on What "Rest" Really Means (2.5 min)

CHAPTER 2

READ
- *What's Your Worldview?: An Interactive Approach to Life's Big Questions* by James Anderson

- *Reading Genesis 1–2: An Evangelical Conversation* by J. Daryl Charles, Richard Averbeck, et al.

LISTEN

- *Pillar Podcast*, "Original Matter Doesn't Matter: Reading Genesis 1 Better," March 16, 2017 (20 min)

WATCH

- BibleProject, "Writing Styles of the Bible & Why They're Important to Understand" (5 min)
- Seedbed, Seven Minute Seminary, "How to Read Genesis 1 in Its Ancient Context—Part 1" with Sandra Richter (7 min)

CHAPTER 3

READ

- *The Epic of Eden: A Christian Entry into the Old Testament* by Sandra Richter

LISTEN

- "Constellations" by Ellie Holcomb on her 2020 album *Canyon* (3.5 min)

WATCH

- BibleProject, "What the Idea of 'Holiness' Means in the Bible" (6.5 min)

CHAPTER 4

READ

- *How to Pray: A Simple Guide for Normal People* by Pete Greig

LISTEN

- *Pillar Podcast*, "The Democratization of Divination," February 18, 2019 (28 min)

- "Too Good" by Jess Ray from her 2015 album *Sentimental Creatures* (4 min)

WATCH

- Seedbed, Seven Minute Seminary, "How to Read Genesis 1 in Its Ancient Context—Part 2" with Sandra Richter (7 min)

CHAPTER 5

READ

- *Prayer in the Night: For Those Who Work or Watch or Weep* by Tish Harrison Warren

LISTEN

- *The GoodHard Story Podcast*, "Episode 25: Redefining Good," June 1, 2023 (34 min)
- "She Waits" by The Gray Havens from their 2018 album *She Waits* (4 min)
- "Clara's Song" by Jenn Alexander from her 2012 album *Walking on the Seam* (4.5 min)

WATCH

- Seedbed, Seven Minute Seminary, "Is Jesus More Loving than God in the Old Testament?" with Sandra Richter (6 min)

CHAPTER 6

READ

- *What If Jesus Was Serious?* by Skye Jethani

LISTEN

- *Pillar Podcast*, "Gods, their babies, and Genesis 1," February 2, 2017 (30 min)

WATCH

- BioLogos, "N. T. Wright on Genesis" (3 min)

CHAPTER 7

READ

- *Being God's Image: Why Creation Still Matters* by Carmen Joy Imes

LISTEN

- "In the Fields of the Lord" (live) [feat. Audrey Assad and Paul Zach] by Porter's Gate on their 2017 album *Work Songs: The Porter's Gate Worship Project* (3 min)

WATCH

- BibleProject, "You're Supposed to Rule the World (Here's How)" (5 min)

CHAPTER 8

READ

- *Surprised by Hope: Rethinking Heaven, the Resurrection, and the Mission of the Church* by N. T. Wright

LISTEN

- "No Bread," 2022 single by Liz Vice (3.5 min)
- "Your Labor Is Not in Vain" (live) [feat. Paul Zach] by Porter's Gate on their 2017 album *Work Songs: The Porter's Gate Worship Project* (4 min)

WATCH

- N. T. Wright Online, "Just How Fallen Is Creation?" *Thinking Through Salvation*, Episode 6 (9 min)

CHAPTER 9

READ

- *A Long Obedience in the Same Direction: Discipleship in an Instant Society* by Eugene Peterson

- *The Screwtape Letters* by C. S. Lewis

LISTEN
- *Pillar Podcast*, "The Curious Case of Cosmic Combat in Creation," March 21, 2018 (20 min)
- "Nothing to Fear" by Paul Zach on his 2022 album *Sorrow's Got a Hold on Me* (3 min)

WATCH
- BibleProject, "What God's Blessing (and Curse) Are All About" (6 min)

CHAPTER 10

READ
- *Bearing God's Name: Why Sinai Still Matters* by Carmen Joy Imes
- *The King Jesus Gospel: The Original Good News Revisited* by Scot McKnight

LISTEN
- *Pillar Podcast*, "Can We Roll on Shabbos?," March 2, 2018 (25 min)
- "The Lord Will Provide" by Jon Guerra on his 2023 album *Ordinary Ways* (4 min)

WATCH
- BibleProject, "What Jesus' Most Well-Known Words Were All About" (5.5 min)

COSMOGONY
QUICK REFERENCE

ANCIENT HISTORY

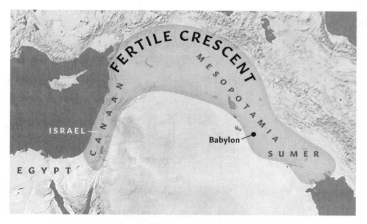

Map used with creative license permission, by Semhur with modification by Rafy and Rachel.

We explore quite a few ancient cosmogonies from across Mesopotamia and into Egypt. If you're a history geek like me or enjoy seeing a map of where things are, keep reading for a simple cheat sheet.

EGYPT

Memphite Theology, Shabako Stone on display at the British Museum, creative common use, Neil Cummings

Title	"Memphite Theology"
Medium	Incised in black granite
Approximate Date	1200 BC[1]
Summary	The god Ptah speaks all things into existence

BABYLON

Epic of Creation (Enuma Elish), one version (Tablet 3) on display at the British Museum, creative common use, Zunkir

Title	Epic of Creation (Enuma Elish)
Medium	cuneiform clay tablet
Approximate Date	1300–1100 BC[2]
Summary	After creation and war, the god Marduk is elevated to the top of the pantheon

Title	Atra-hasis
Medium	cuneiform clay tablet, one copy displayed at the British Museum
Approximate Date	1600 BC[3]
Summary	Creation of man and the purpose of man

SUMER

Title	Eridu Genesis
Medium	cuneiform clay tablet, one copy on display at the Penn Museum
Approximate Date	1600 BC[4]
Summary	The gods created Sumerians and built cities, followed by a flood

Title	Enki and Ninmah
Medium	cuneiform clay tablet, tablets currently held at the Penn Museum
Approximate Date	1900–1600 BC[5]
Summary	The creation of man and a contest with another god

TWENTY-FIRST-CENTURY QUESTIONS

Why not just give the ancient Israelites a scientific account that would demonstrate how omniscient God is?

The Principle of Accommodation, developed by Reformation theologian John Calvin, helps us make sense of this issue. In essence, this principle means that God reveals parts of who He is to us in ways we are able to comprehend. If God were to overwhelm the Israelites with scientific data that would only be understood thousands of years later, they would likely lose the forest for the trees (as would we!). Rather, God meets people where they are and then pushes the envelope just enough to reveal *who* He is.

Theologian Alister McGrath explains the principle further: "The analogy which lies behind Calvin's thinking at this point is that of a human orator. Good speakers know the limitations of their audience and adjust the way they speak accordingly. The gulf between the speaker and the hearer must be bridged if communication is to take place. God has to come down to our level in the process of revelation."[1]

Good software developers use this principle. It's the most efficient use of everyone's time to start communication at the level of the listener. This is why your computer software uses the terms "desktop" and "file." You already know what those are in the physical world and transfer that understanding into organizing your digital world.

If you think back on your life, you've likely seen this principle in action. When you first began to walk with Christ, did you find yourself overwhelmed with every conviction you now follow? Likely, it started with one or two truths that permeated your soul, and as you matured, He showed you more of His character.

God did the same for the Israelites. It may take us a bit more work (and humility!) to dig and find the truths God was showering on His people, but it's worth the effort. God's truths always are.

Does Genesis teach "creatio ex nihilo" (creation from nothing)?

Dr. Janet Soskice, a professor at Duke Divinity School, provides a helpful working definition for the Latin phrase: "*creatio ex nihilo* affirms that God, from no compulsion or necessity, created the world out of nothing—really nothing—no preexistent matter, space, or time."[2] This church doctrine first appeared in the Second Temple period (1 Macc. 7:28) and was then picked up by the church as a foundational teaching by the mid-300s AD,[3] and stems from Colossians 1:15–17:

> He is the image of the invisible God, the firstborn of all creation. For by Him all things were created, both in the heavens and on earth, visible and invisible, whether thrones or dominions or rulers or authorities—all things have been created through Him and for Him. He is before all things, and in Him all things hold together.

As was discussed in chapter 4, Genesis seems to begin creation with a need to organize matter already in existence. Dr. Tremper Longman, professor of Biblical Studies at Westmont College, notes that the Hebrew grammar in Genesis 1 is vague concerning "when" God began creation (i.e., was it before or after the matter existed?).[4] He goes on to say:

> Later biblical texts clearly teach that God created everything, so the biblical doctrine of creation from nothing stands secure. It is likely, however, that the author of Genesis 1 was simply not interested in the question of the origin of matter. That becomes a question in the later Greco-Roman environment. I imagine that if the author of Genesis were asked where the matter came from, he would answer that of course God created it.[5]

To answer the question, "Does Genesis teach creation *ex nihilo*?" I would say, not explicitly (as in the book of Colossians). But Genesis does not undermine the doctrine either. Genesis can agree with *creatio ex nihilo* in that it doesn't address *ex nihilo* at all, neither endorsing nor contradicting it.

Is Genesis 1–2:3 describing literal twenty-four-hour days?

This is a common question among evangelicals, and it is fair because the text says "one day," counting up to seven days. My short answer is: sure, it could be. There is no reason that Genesis 1–2:3 is not describing seven days, as a day is commonly measured in twenty-four-hour increments. However, the better question is to ask *why* God uses seven days? Hopefully, chapter 3 elucidated an answer. When we hear "one day," we quickly jump to questions of time. Perhaps the men and women in ANE cultures would have wondered that as well, but I think *why* Genesis counted days was of much larger significance to them. As the first verses of Genesis were told around a campfire, I picture a small smile and curious head tilt of the ANE Israelite as they leaned in to hear the next special and sacred thing God would do. What would happen on day two? How many days was this going to go?

The answers to the *why* questions are longer, a little more work, and certainly humbling because my answer is usually, "I have no idea . . . yet!" I find these why questions lead to tension and even frustration sometimes but it is within that wrestling that I grow to trust God and His character more and more. The book you hold in your hands is the result of much wrestling and research, an attempt to find answers deeper than "just because." To be honest, sometimes, it's scary to do the work to discover why God says what He does because I might not like the answer. Even when I do like the answer, it is inevitably followed by conviction because God is always bigger and more generous than I can anticipate.

This is the path of faith and discipleship, friends. I'm glad you're asking the why questions right alongside me.

How was there light before there was a sun?

From a literature standpoint, there are two thoughts about why light existed before the sun in Genesis. First, on day one, the mixing of light and dark was representative of chaos. As discussed in chapter 4, the combining of elements that should be separate—like the mixing of salt and fresh water in *Epic of Creation (Enuma Elish)*—was a clear indication of chaos. The separation of light and dark demonstrated God's ability to bring order to chaos. It was step one in providing structural organization to the cosmos. When the sun and moon appeared on day four, they are providing a purpose within the order God had begun to organize on day one.

A second reason that light came before the sun can be understood by examining ANE culture's understanding of time. John Walton suggests that on day one when God separated light and dark, He was creating time.[6] This theory fits with the Egyptians' concept of time. They incorporated an eternal timeline and a cyclical earthbound sense of time (seen in years, seasons, and aging).[7]

As ancient cultures were concerned with purpose, the separation of light and dark on day one would establish the beginning of eternal time. To continue with this theory, the installation of the sun and moon on day four would have marked the beginning of the seasonal cycles on earth. God directly states the purpose for the sun and moon as indicators for seasons when He says, "Let them be signs to mark the seasons, days, and years" (Gen. 1:14b NLT).

Either of the stated reasons can help make sense of the timeline in the biblical account of creation. Remember, though, that the ancient Near Eastern men and women were more concerned with the purpose of creation, not the actual matter or process of creation. God was working within the way they understood both time and light and declaring Himself ruler over it all.

ACKNOWLEDGMENTS

This book started in a Torah class taught by Dr. Eric Smith at Pillar Seminary. During class discussions, I sat on Zoom with my mouth open and felt like I was barely keeping my head afloat. Dr. Smith answered my ridiculous questions and waded through my reading summaries, guiding me to better understand Genesis 1–12. Years later, he graciously read copies of my chapters and offered feedback on the technical details. Dr. Smith has always encouraged me to do my best and pushed me to treat the Bible with integrity and honor. I am thankful for his investment in the seminary and his students, and I count myself privileged to be among them.

As I began writing, Dr. Scott Booth replied to my texts, FaceTimes, and emailed ANE questions without fail. Whether his support was because I'm his older sister or because I have been his student, it was invaluable to me. He's known among his students to be an expert and unendingly patient in helping us get to the truth of Scripture. I can say his reputation carries to his family too. I know of no one more dedicated to making the Bible accessible. The drawings by his daughter, Lucy, came in clutch for chapter 8 too. Nice work, Lucy!

While at Pillar Seminary, Dr. Donnell Moore impressed on us that our studies aided our spiritual calling, not our ego or growing bookshelves. Slowly and with a smile, he helped me learn to incorporate my spiritual gifts, calling, and education—all for God's glory. He worked hard to keep us from becoming noisy gongs, and I'm forever grateful.

I was fortunate that one of my first Bible teachers was Deb Jordan. Her passion for the Bible and corresponding insistence on intellectual honesty greatly imprinted on me. Cancer is a beast and took you too soon. You are missed, Deb. Gina Rodriguez was the first person to tell me I could teach and write, and then she assigned me a classroom to do just that. Gina, I am so humbled you gave me the freedom and setting to flourish. Lindsay May and her magazine *Truly Co.* allowed me space to write theologically, and Tonya Melody encouraged me to keep moving toward publishing. Thank you for your affirmations and encouragement.

Getting a book to the publishing stage is no joke, and I have Glynnis Whitwear, Meredith Brock, and Kat Armstrong to thank for their insights, coaching, and networking. I'm grateful Trillia Newbell passed my proposal to Catherine Parks. I'm even more grateful Catherine took a chance on an author who couldn't get an agent and whose social media is just socially awkward. Thanks for taking a chance on *Rest Assured*. And thanks to Ashleigh Slater for her editing insight and help in making *Rest Assured* tight and strong. Moody Publishers has been gracious and wonderful to work with; I feel so honored to have partnered with them.

Amy Philibeck, friend and fellow Pillar student, got the ideas for a study about creation humming and gave me a running start. I'm so thankful to the advanced readers who made excellent suggestions, especially to friend and editor extraordinaire Jen Allee, who walked with me every. single. step. Jen, your insights, wisdom, and encouragement have meant the world to me. And to my dear boot camp buddies—Leslie McCleod, Amy Lively, Peggy Bodde, and Jessica Hanna—you are a blessing beyond measure. I loved writing the proposal for this book alongside you all, but I have loved our friendship more. You are fantastic.

A few years ago, a group of women started meeting at my house for a book club that wasn't afraid to delve into theology, hot topics, and current events. I learned so much from each of the women who attended. Your deep questions and thoughtful exchanges were life-giving to me in a season of drought, and I am forever thankful for each of you.

To Loren Latourelle, Hillary Leeper, Lucita Lepisto, Joy Herzog, Teresa Swanson, Betsy Beach, and Emily Hannah—you have each supported me and cheered me on. Writing can be lonely and full of rejection, and you sat with me and acknowledged the loneliness and rejection while also never letting me stay there. With kindness, coffee, and laughs, you helped me find my footing, my lane, and the finish line. I love you all more than I can express. Thank you.

Mom and Dad, you have cheered me on and never tired of my questions (at least to my face). You helped me overcome my learning differences and shrugged off teachers who were too short-sighted to imagine a world with spell-check. I have never wondered if you thought I could accomplish something (even though I was sure I couldn't). Over and over, I have borrowed your confidence, which seems to be a marker of great parents. Thank you, and I love you very much.

Stephen, Clara, and Abbie—you have graciously shared your lives and stories on these pages. Thank you for sharing your mom as I typed away instead of making dinner. Thanks, too, for listening to ANE facts and theology discussions over takeout. You're all troupers, and I adore you.

I am a girl used to big feelings, but my love for Brian Smith since I was seventeen has put my other emotions to shame. Brian, thank you for your patience, kindness, easygoing nature, patience, generosity, care, encouragement, and . . . patience. I can't imagine what I did to find myself with such an amazing guy, but I never want to take it for granted. None of these pages would have been written without your support, and I'm so grateful for a husband who loves to see his wife thrive. I'm crazy about you and so thankful to be yours.

And all thanks to my dear Savior, Jesus. You have orchestrated all the events in these acknowledgments, placing all these lovely people in my life. More than that, You've gifted me with Your presence, love, kindness, and faithfulness my whole life. It's astounding. I pray a bit of the love You've shown me leaks through these pages, and I pray the words I've written provide a glimpse of Your trustworthy nature. I love You.

NOTES

CHAPTER 1: RESTLESS HEARTS

Epigraph: Maltbie Babcock, "This Is My Father's World," in *The United Methodist Hymnal: Book of United Methodist Worship*, 7 (Nashville: United Methodist Publishing House, 1989), 144.

1. "Restless," track 5 on Audrey Assad, *The House You're Building*, Sparrow, 2010. Copyright © 2010 Thankyou Music Ltd (PRS) (adm. worldwide at CapitolCMGPublishing.com excluding the UK & Europe, which is adm. at IntegratedRights.com) / Valley of Songs Music (BMI) River Oaks Music Company (BMI) (adm. at CapitolCMGPublishing.com). All rights reserved. Used by permission.

2. Augustine, *The Confessions*, ed. John E. Rotelle, trans. Maria Boulding, *The Works of Saint Augustine: A Translation for the 21st Century, Part 1: Books*, vol. 1 (Hyde Park, NY: New City Press, 1997), 39.

3. Seminomadic pastoralists lived in villages in the summer and traveled with their flocks in the winter. See Marc Van De Mieroop, *A History of the Ancient Near East ca. 3000–323 BC*, 3rd ed., Blackwell History of the Ancient World (Chichester, England: Wiley Blackwell, 2016), 92–95. Nomads such as Abraham traveled from Ur (present-day Iraq) to Harran (present-day Turkey) to Canaan (present-day Israel) to Egypt (see Gen. 11:27–32; 12:10). Between the widespread travel in the ANE and the discovery of texts across regions (see chapter 1, note 11), it is reasonable to expect that these stories would be told in cities and the countryside, not isolated to their country of origin.

4. In Egypt, the "Memphite Theology" says, "So has Ptah come to rest after his making everything . . ." James P. Allen, "From the 'Memphite Theology' (1.15)," in *The Context of Scripture*, ed. William W. Hallo and K. Lawson Younger (Leiden, Netherlands: Brill, 2003), 1:23. (For specific lines, see the role of Ptah [cols 58–61].) In the Babylonian creation account *Enuma Elish*, Marduk kills other gods and then completes creation. The other gods tell him, "We shall lay out the shrine, let us set up its emplacement/When we come (to visit you), we shall find rest therein." Benjamin R. Foster, "Epic of Creation (1.111) (Enuma Elish)," in *The Context of Scripture*, ed. William W. Hallo and K. Lawson Younger (Leiden: Brill, 2003), 1:401. (For specific verses, see lines 53–54.) In a Ugaritic myth about Ba'al (Ba'lu), after a great battle, a god sings, "Let them place Ba'lu [on] his royal [throne], on [(his) resting-place, on the seat of] his dominion." Dennis Pardee, "The Ba'lu Myth (1.86)," in *The Context of Scripture*, ed. William W. Hallo and K. Lawson Younger (Leiden: Brill, 2003), 1:273. (For specific lines, see Motu Capitulates [vi 30–?].)

5. John H. Walton, *Genesis 1 as Ancient Cosmology* (Winona Lake, IN: Eisenbrauns, 2011), 110.

6. John H. Walton, *Ancient Near Eastern Thought and the Old Testament: Introducing the Conceptual World of the Hebrew Bible*, 2nd ed. (Grand Rapids, MI: Baker Academic, 2018), 73.

7. In cosmogonies and other ancient texts, gods *do* sleep, but the concept is very similar to that of rest. Dr. Batto says that "to judge from the literature of the ancient Near East, the motif of the sleeping deity actually involves several related concepts . . . A) rest as a divine prerogative, and B) sleeping as a symbol of divine rule." Bernard F. Batto, "The Sleeping God: An Ancient Near Eastern Motif of Divine Sovereignty," *Biblica* 68, no. 2 (1987): 155–56.

8. John H. Walton, "Interpreting the Bible as an Ancient Near Eastern Document," in *Israel: Ancient Kingdom or Late Invention?*, ed. Daniel I. Block (Nashville: B&H Academic Group, 2008), 325.

9. They might belong in the John 1:1–5 or Colossians 1:15–17 rooms, books written to a Greek culture more aligned with the twenty-first-century Western worldview.

10. I like how Dr. Gordon Wenham, Old Testament scholar at Trinity University, talks about the distraction of the science versus Bible debate. "Instead of reading the chapter as a triumphant affirmation of the power and wisdom of God and the wonder of his creation, we have been too often bogged down in attempting to squeeze Scripture into the mold of the latest scientific hypothesis or distorting scientific facts to fit a particular interpretation. When allowed to speak for itself, Gen 1 looks beyond such minutiae. Its proclamation of the God of grace and power who undergirds the world and gives it purpose justifies the scientific approach to nature." Gordon J. Wenham, *Genesis 1–15*, Word Biblical Commentary (Waco, TX: Word Books, 1987), 40.

11. I am aware of the authorship issues regarding Genesis 1–2:3. I have chosen to approach the text canonically (as a complete text passed down and received).

12. Stories such as "Epic of Gilgamesh" (a poem about finding eternal life from Sumer [modern-day Iraq]), dated as early as Abraham's time, were found in Israel (Megiddo). Wayne Horowitz, Takayoshi Oshima, and Seth Sanders, *Cuneiform in Canaan: Cuneiform Sources from the Land of Israel in Ancient Times* (Jerusalem: Israel Exploration Society, 2006), 102. Literary works written in Akkadian were found in the Amarna letters—an archive in Egypt dated to the second millennium BC. Horowitz, Oshima, and Sanders, *Cuneiform in Canaan*, 16.

13. Walton, *Ancient Near Eastern Thought and the Old Testament*, 47.

14. As an example of this mindset, Dr. Averbeck notes in his study of Enki and the World Order that "Enki's careful *supernatural* attention to the Sumerian world order had yielded a full and abundant *natural* restoration of Sumer." Richard E. Averbeck, "Myth, Ritual, and Order in 'Enki and the World Order,'" *Journal of the American Oriental Society* 123, no. 4 (October–December 2003): 771.

15. Augustine, *The Confessions*, 39.

16. Parts of this chapter first appeared in the following article: Rachel Booth Smith, "If Troubled, Look for God's Comfort. If Restless, Look for His Lordship," *Christianity Today*, December 2022, 56–61.

CHAPTER 2: MORE THAN A STORY

Epigraph: Thomas O. Chisholm, "Great Is Thy Faithfulness," in *The United Methodist Hymnal: Book of United Methodist Worship*, 7 (Nashville: United Methodist Publishing House, 1989), 140.

1. Scholars struggle to agree on a genre label for Genesis 1. The features are unique enough that it is difficult to place it solidly within our modern genre definitions. Within the book *Reading Genesis 1–2: An Evangelical Conversation*, Old Testament experts spend much time debating exactly how to classify the first chapters of the Bible. Averbeck says, "Gen 1–2 constitute observational cosmogony and cosmology" (p. 31), Collins calls it "exalted prose narrative" (p. 86), Beal states it is "a literal, historical account" (p. 57), Longmann calls it "theological history" (p. 110), and Walton sees it as "cosmology" (p. 145). For the purposes of our study, I fall closest to Dr. Averbeck and Dr. Walton's view and will be defining Genesis 1–2 as a cosmogony while using the *Dictionary of the Old Testament* as a reference point. For those who would like to dig deeper into this issue and understand the intricacies of the debate, I highly recommend *Reading Genesis 1–2: An Evangelical Conversation*. J. Daryl Charles, ed. *Reading Genesis 1–2: An Evangelical Conversation* (Peabody, MA: Hendrickson Publishers, 2013).

2. The words *cosmogony* and *cosmology* are tied closely together. Lucas's explanation is helpful: "Cosmology refers to the understanding of the whole universe as an organized, structured entity. Strictly speaking it can be distinguished from cosmogony, which is an account of how the structured universe came into being. However, it is difficult to separate these two, since cosmologies are often rooted in cosmogonies. The way a universe *is* is seen to be dependent on the way *it came into being*." E. C. Lucas, "Cosmology," in *Dictionary of the Old Testament: Pentateuch*, ed. T. Desmond Alexander and David W. Baker (Downers Grove, IL: InterVarsity Press, 2003), 130.

3. Lucas, "Cosmology," 130.

4. Dr. Averbeck writes, "In Gen 1 we watch God paint his literary picture of creation and the cosmos step by step, and he paints it against the same standard backdrop as would be normal in the ancient Near East. The picture itself is quite different in many important aspects, but there

are also other similarities to ANE accounts." Richard E. Averbeck, "A Literary Day, Inter-Textual, and Contextual Reading of Genesis 1–2," in *Reading Genesis 1–2: An Evangelical Conversation*, ed. J. Daryl Charles (Peabody, MA: Hendrickson Publishers, 2013), 12.

5. Lucas, "Cosmology," 130–31.

6. Dr. Hoffmeier, Old Testament scholar and Egyptologist, argues that the influence of Egypt on the Israelites also would have been strong. In his article, he notes, "The Israelites had their origins somewhere in Syria-Mesopotamia. Even after the sojourn in Egypt, Joshua recalled their origins as being 'beyond the Euphrates' (Josh. 24:2)." James K. Hoffmeier, "Some Thoughts on Genesis 1 & 2 and Egyptian Cosmology," *The Journal of the Ancient Near Eastern Society* 15 (1983): 48.

CHAPTER 3: BEGINNING AT THE END

1. James P. Allen, "From the 'Memphite Theology' (1.15)," in *The Context of Scripture*, ed. William W. Hallo and K. Lawson Younger (Leiden: Brill, 2003), 1:23. Note: *nomes* were territorial divisions of ancient Egypt (see lines in the role of Ptah).

2. Richard E. Averbeck, "The Cylinders of Gudea (2.155)," in *The Context of Scripture*, ed. William W. Hallo and K. Lawson Younger (Leiden: Brill, 2003), 2:432. (See Cyl. Bxix.18–21.)

3. Benjamin R. Foster, "Epic of Creation (1.111) (Enuma Elish)," in *The Context of Scripture*, ed. William W. Hallo and K. Lawson Younger (Leiden: Brill, 2003), 401. (See lines 70–79.)

4. Foster, "Epic of Creation," 401. (See lines 53–54; 78–80.)

5. Nahum M. Sarna, *Exploring Exodus: The Heritage of Biblical Israel* (New York: Schocken Books, 1986), 147.

6. Michael V. Fox, "Papyrus Chester Beatty I (1.51)," in *The Context of Scripture*, ed. William W. Hallo and K. Lawson Younger (Leiden: Brill, 2003), 1:129. (See end of seventh stanza.)

7. Daniel Fleming, "The Installation of the Storm God's High Priestess (1.122)," in *The Context of Scripture*, ed. William W. Hallo and K. Lawson Younger (Leiden: Brill, 2003), 1:427–431. (Seven is an important number throughout the ceremony.)

8. There has been an excellent study done (by Dr. John Walton [Walton, *Genesis 1 as Ancient Cosmology*, 100–121] and Dr. Jon Levenson [Jon D. Levenson, "The Temple and the World," *The Journal of Religion* 64, no. 3 (1984): 275–98] in particular) to suggest that Genesis 1 describes a cosmic temple dedication ceremony. I appreciate their research but am persuaded by Dr. Richard Averbeck's argument that though the dedication ceremony may be a point of reference in Genesis, the direct correlation to a temple ceremony is difficult to apply (J. Daryl Charles, ed., *Reading Genesis 1–2: An Evangelical Conversation* [Peabody, MA: Hendrickson Publishers 2013], 170–72.). One view says the cosmos *is* a temple; the other says it is *like* a temple. I find both compelling but tend to have more alignment with the latter.

9. E. C. Lucas writes, "Religious cosmogonies normally involve personal entities—the God or gods—who have aims and purposes and values. Their primary purpose is not to provide factual information about the past history of the physical universe but to ground or explain particular aspects of present reality." Lucas, "Cosmology," in *Dictionary of the Old Testament: Pentateuch*, ed. T. Desmond Alexander and David W. Baker (Downers Grove, IL: InterVarsity Press, 2003), 131.

CHAPTER 4: SPEAKING TO CHAOS

Epigraph: Maltbie Babcock, "This Is My Father's World," in *The United Methodist Hymnal: Book of United Methodist Worship*, 7 (Nashville: United Methodist Publishing House, 1989), 144.

1. Benjamin R. Foster, "Epic of Creation (1.111) (Enuma Elish)," in *The Context of Scripture*, ed. William W. Hallo and K. Lawson Younger (Leiden: Brill, 2003), 391 (see Tablet I, lines 1–8).

2. John H. Walton, "Reading Genesis 1 as Ancient Cosmology," in *Reading Genesis 1–2: An Evangelical Conversation*, ed. J. Daryl Charles (Peabody, MA: Hendrickson Publishers, 2013), 148.

3. Foster, "Epic of Creation," 391 (see Tablet I, lines 9–16).

4. Foster, "Epic of Creation," 391 (see Tablet I, lines 20–28).

5. Foster, "Epic of Creation," 391. Apsu summons a vizier to counsel him (see Tablet I, lines 29–34).

6. Foster, "Epic of Creation," 393–94. Anshar, Ea's father, offers good advice to Ea (see Tablet II, lines 47–54). Nudimmud offers good advice to Anshar (see Tablet II, lines 57–70).

7. Foster, "Epic of Creation," 391–92. Mummu is a bad advisor, advising Apsu to kill his children (other gods; see Tablet I, lines 47–54). The gods as a group are also bad advisors, urging Tiamat to destroy Ea (see Tablet I, lines 110–132).

8. Foster, "Epic of Creation," 391, 397. Ea brings order by using a magic spell to kill Apsu (see Tablet I, lines 62–69). Marduk commands constellations destroyed and created (see Tablet IV, lines 25–26).

9. Foster, "Epic of Creation," 391, 393. Both Ea (see Tablet I, lines 59–62) and Nudimmud (see Tablet II, lines 57–60) are praised for their wisdom.

10. Foster, "Epic of Creation," 391, 398. Ea kills Apsu while Apsu is sleeping and binds Mummu (see Tablet I, lines 65–70). Marduk fights Tiamat in a climactic duel, resulting in Tiamat being split in two (see Tablet IV, lines 87–139).

11. Foster, "Epic of Creation," 391 (see Tablet I, lines 1–2).

12. Walter Farber, "Witchcraft, Magic, and Divination in Ancient Mesopotamia," in *Civilizations of the Ancient Near East I–IV*, ed. Jack M. Sasson (New York: Scribner, 1995), 1895.

13. Benjamin R. Foster, "The Poem of the Righteous Sufferer (1.153)," in *The Context of Scripture*, ed. William W. Hallo and K. Lawson Younger (Leiden: Brill, 2003) 1:487 (see Tablet I).

14. "In the Egyptian view, all that now exists began as a unity, a primordial Monad–Atum–floating in the dark, lifeless infinity of pre-creation ('the Flood, the Waters, Chaos and Darkness')." James P. Allen, "Genesis in Egypt: The Philosophy of Ancient Egyptian Creation Accounts," in *Yale Egyptological Studies 2*, ed. William K. Simpson (New Haven, CT: Yale University Press, 1988), 24.

15. Atum creates Shu and Tefnut with his semen. James P. Allen, "From Pyramid Texts Spell 527 (1.3)," in *The Context of Scripture*, ed. William W. Hallo and K. Lawson Younger (Leiden: Brill, 2003) 1:7. The god Atum creates the god Shu with a sneeze and the god Tefnut with spit.

James P. Allen, "The Pyramid Texts Spell 600 (1.4)," in *The Context of Scripture*, ed. William W. Hallo and K. Lawson Younger (Leiden: Brill, 2003) 1:7.

16. Allen, "Genesis in Egypt: The Philosophy of Ancient Egyptian Creation Accounts," 24.

17. James P. Allen, *Middle Egyptian: An Introduction to the Language and Culture of Hieroglyphs*, 2nd ed. (Cambridge: Cambridge University Press, 2010), 160.

18. James P. Allen, "From Coffin Texts Spell 80 (1.8)," in *The Context of Scripture*, ed. William W. Hallo and K. Lawson Younger (Leiden: Brill, 2003), 1:12–13. "Then said Atum to the waters" (see bottom page 12), "The Waters said to Atum" (see top of page 13).

19. Allen, "Genesis in Egypt: The Philosophy of Ancient Egyptian Creation Accounts," 61.

20. James P. Allen, "From Papyrus Lieden I 350 (1.16)," in *The Context of Scripture*, ed. William W. Hallo and K. Lawson Younger (Leiden: Brill, 2003), 1:24 (see 90th chapter).

21. Allen, *Middle Egyptian*, 161. Allen has a helpful definition here: "Perception is the ability to see what needs to be done, and annunciation is the power to make it happen through speech. The king's courtiers say to him, for example, 'Annunciation is in your mouth, perception is in your heart: your speech is the shrine of Maat" (KRI II, 356, 9–11).

22. Allen, "Genesis in Egypt: The Philosophy of Ancient Egyptian Creation Accounts," 38.

23. Herman te Velde, "Theology, Priests, and Worship in Ancient Egypt," in *Civilizations of the Ancient Near East I–IV*, ed. Jack M. Sasson (New York: Scribner, 1995), 1748.

24. te Velde, "Theology, Priests, and Worship in Ancient Egypt," 1747.

25. te Velde, "Theology, Priests, and Worship in Ancient Egypt," 1748.

26. The categories are elucidated as "individual features" in Walton's creation entry in the *Dictionary of the Old Testament: Pentateuch*. John H. Walton, "Creation," in *Dictionary of the Old Testament: Pentateuch*,

ed. T. Desmond Alexander and David W. Baker (Downers Grove, IL: InterVarsity Press, 2003), 156–62.

27. Tom Wright, *The Lord and His Prayer* (Great Britain: BPC Paperbacks Ltd., 1996), 2.

28. Pete Greig, *How to Pray: A Simple Guide for Normal People* (Colorado Springs: NavPress, 2019), 15.

CHAPTER 5: INCONCEIVABLE!

1. James P. Allen, "From Coffin Texts Spell 76 (1.6)," in *The Context of Scripture*, ed. William W. Hallo and K. Lawson Younger (Leiden: Brill, 2003), 1:10 (see CTII 2b–3c).

2. Rita Lucarelli, "God's, Spirits, and Demons of the Book of the Dead," in *Book of the Dead: Becoming God in Ancient Egypt*, ed. Foy Scalf (Chicago: The Oriental Institute of the University of Chicago, 2017), 129.

3. Benjamin R. Foster, "Epic of Creation (1.111) (Enuma Elish)," in *The Context of Scripture*, ed. William W. Hallo and K. Lawson Younger (Leiden: Brill, 2003), 398 (see Tablet IV, lines 93–94; 129–131; 137–141).

4. See Exodus 24:9–11. In this astounding event, Moses, Aaron, Aaron's sons, and seventy elders went up to heaven and had dinner with God (a lovely communion after being sprinkled with the blood of the covenant). The blue under God's feet fits as a depiction of the dome, expanse, or רקיע (rāqîaʿ) under their feet.

5. Ludwig Koehler and Walter Baumgartner, eds., *Hebrew and Aramaic Lexicon of the Old Testament: Study Edition* (Leiden: Brill, 2001), s.v. "רקיע," 1290.

6. Sandra L. Richter, *The Epic of Eden: A Christian Entry into the Old Testament* (Downers Grove, IL: IVP Academic, 2008), 102.

7. Mark Smith notes in his book *The Priestly Vision of Genesis 1* that this arrangement can be traced to Johann Gottfried von Herder. Mark Smith, *The Priestly Vision of Genesis 1* (Minneapolis: Fortress Press, 2010), 253 (see note #17).

8. John H. Walton, *Genesis: From Biblical Text . . . to Contemporary Life*, The NIV Application Commentary (Grand Rapids, MI: Zondervan, 2001), 116.

9. Walton, *Genesis*, 115.

10. See also Job 9:8; Psalm 77:19; and Habakkuk 3:15.

11. See also Psalms 65:7; 89:9; 107:29.

12. Horatio G. Spafford, "It Is Well with My Soul," in *The United Methodist Hymnal: Book of United Methodist Worship*, 7 (Nashville: United Methodist Publishing House, 1989), 377.

13. The psalmist compares deep waters with trouble (Pss. 18:16–17; 144:7–8) and distress (Ps. 69:1–4, 14–18).

CHAPTER 6: WHAT'S IN A NAME?

Epigraph: Maltbie Babcock, "This Is My Father's World," in *The United Methodist Hymnal: Book of United Methodist Worship*, 7 (Nashville: United Methodist Publishing House, 1989), 144.

1. John H. Walton, *Genesis: From Biblical Text . . . to Contemporary Life*, The NIV Application Commentary (Grand Rapids, MI: Zondervan, 2001), 158.

2. Benjamin R. Foster, "Epic of Creation (1.111) (Enuma Elish)," in *The Context of Scripture*, ed. William W. Hallo and K. Lawson Younger (Leiden: Brill, 2003), 391 (see Tablet I, lines 1–2).

3. John H. Walton, "Reading Genesis 1 as Ancient Cosmology," in *Reading Genesis 1–2: An Evangelical Conversation*, ed. J. Daryl Charles (Peabody, MA: Hendrickson Publishers, 2013), 165.

4. Another example of the naming principle happens when God changes Abram's name to Abraham when his "function" changes. "No longer shall your name be called Abram, But your name shall be Abraham; For I have made you the father of a multitude of nations" (Gen. 17:5).

5. Foster, "Epic of Creation," 399 (see Tablet V, lines 1–8).

6. J. David Schloen, *The House of the Father as Fact and Symbol: Patrimonialism in Ugarit and the Ancient Near East*, Studies in the Archaeology and History of the Levant 2 (Winona Lake, IN: Eisenbrauns, 2001), 91, 255.

7. Janice Polonsky, "The Rise of the Sun God and the Determination of Destiny in Ancient Mesopotamia" (PhD, University of Pennsylvania, 2002), 1019–20.

8. Gordon J. Wenham, *Exploring the Old Testament: A Guide to the Pentateuch*, Exploring the Bible Series, vol. 1 (Downers Grove, IL: InterVarsity Press, 2008), 16.

9. E. C. Lucas, "Cosmology," in *Dictionary of the Old Testament: Pentateuch*, ed. T. Desmond Alexander and David W. Baker (Downers Grove, IL: InterVarsity Press, 2003), 134.

10. Adopting another god's character was not uncommon. "They co-opt the competencies of the other gods as needed, offering in one place what the other gods offer corporately. The goal is to justify their supremacy, not eliminate the competition, deny their potency, or monopolize their worship." Michael Hundley, *Yahweh Among the Gods: The Divine in Genesis, Exodus, and the Ancient Near East* (Cambridge: Cambridge University Press, 2022), 198. Marduk employs this in *Enuma Elish*. However, in Genesis 1–2:3, God is eliminating the competition, denying their potency, and monopolizing their worship.

11. See Psalms 84:11; 94:1–2.

12. Mark S. Smith, *The Origins of Biblical Monotheism: Israel's Polytheistic Background and the Ugaritic Texts* (New York: Oxford University Press, 2001), 170–71.

13. Job 31:26–28; 2 Kings 23:4; Ezekiel 8:16.

14. Richard E. Averbeck, "Ancient Near Eastern Mythography as It Relates to Historiography in the Hebrew Bible: Genesis 3 and the Cosmic Battle," in *The Future of Biblical Archaeology: Reassessing Methodologies and Assumptions: The Proceedings of a Symposium, August 12–14, 2001 at Trinity International University*, ed. James Karl Hoffmeier and A. R. Millard (Grand Rapids, MI: Eerdmans, 2004), 343.

CHAPTER 7: MADE IN THE IMAGE

Epigraph: Maltbie Babcock, "This Is My Father's World," in *The United Methodist Hymnal: Book of United Methodist Worship*, 7 (Nashville: United Methodist Publishing House, 1989), 144.

1. J. David Schloen, *The House of the Father as Fact and Symbol: Patrimonialism in Ugarit and the Ancient Near East*, Studies in the Archaeology and History of the Levant 2 (Winona Lake, IN: Eisenbrauns, 2001), 152–54.

2. The translation quoted has a (?) here, denoting uncertainty in the translation. "Planned" or "designed" would also be appropriate translations. Eric Smith, PhD, Trinity College, in conversation with author, May 15, 2023.

3. Jacob Klein, "Enki and Ninmah (1.159)," in *The Context of Scripture*, ed. William W. Hallo and K. Lawson Younger (Leiden: Brill, 2003), 1:517. (See lines 28–30.)

4. Bernard F. Batto, *In the Beginning: Essays on Creation Motifs in the Ancient Near East and the Bible*, Siphrut: Literature and Theology of the Hebrew Scriptures 9 (Winona Lake, IN: Eisenbrauns, 2013), 27.

5. Miriam Lichtheim, "Merikare (1.35)," in *The Context of Scripture*, ed. William W. Hallo and K. Lawson Younger (Leiden: Brill, 2003), 1:65. (See line 130.)

6. *Merikare* and another Egyptian text, *Instruction of Ani*, both seem to call all of humanity an "image of god," but as Middleton expresses in his book, these two texts are "distinctly atypical texts, proposing ideas that were common in Egypt only when applied to the pharaoh, not to the mass of humanity . . ." Richard J. Middleton, *The Liberating Image: The Imago Dei in Genesis 1* (Grand Rapids, MI: Brazos Press, 2005), 64.

7. My model is built from the information in Dr. Schloen's excellent work on how a household operated in the ANE. Schloen, *The House of the Father as Fact and Symbol*, 255–313.

8. The gods make other gods. "Then Anu begot his own image Nudimmud." Foster, "Epic of Creation (Enuma Elish) (1.111)," 391 (see Tablet I, line 16).

9. Catherine L. McDowell, *The Image of God in the Garden of Eden: The Creation of Humankind in Genesis 2:5–3:24 in Light of the Mīs Pî Pīt Pî and Wpt-r Rituals of Mesopotamia and Ancient Egypt*, Siphrut: Literature and Theology of the Hebrew Scriptures 15 (Winona Lake, IN: Eisenbrauns, 2015), 118–19.

10. McDowell, *The Image of God*, 85.

11. This prayer of a Hittite king on behalf of his people who are enduring a plague demonstrates how the Hittites viewed the gods needing their support: *[Let] the plague [be removed] from Hatti. Send [it] to the enemy lands. In Hatti [. . .] If you, the gods, my lords, [do not send] the plague [away] from Hatti, the bakers of offering bread and the libation bearers [will die]. And if they die off, [the offering bread] and the libation will be cut off for the gods, [my lords]. Then you will come to me, O gods, [my lords], and hold this (to be) a sin [on my part] (saying): "Why [don't you give] us offering bread and libation?"* Gary Beckman, "Plague Prayers of Mursili II (1.60)," in *The Context of Scripture*, ed. William W. Hallo and K. Lawson Younger (Leiden: Brill, 2003), 1:159 (in Third Prayer, rev. 2'–14'). See also Gary Beckman, "How Religion Was Done," in *A Companion to the Ancient Near East*, ed. Daniel C. Snell (Malden, MA: Blackwell, 2005), 346.

12. Bernard F. Batto, *In the Beginning: Essays on Creation Motifs in the Ancient Near East and the Bible*, Siphrut: Literature and Theology of the Hebrew Scriptures 9 (Winona Lake, IN: Eisenbrauns, 2013), 114.

13. Beckman, "How Religion Was Done," 345–46.

14. Batto, *In the Beginning*, 133.

CHAPTER 8: RESTORATION PARTICIPATION

Epigraph: Charles Wesley, "O for a Thousand Tongues to Sing," in *The United Methodist Hymnal: Book of United Methodist Worship*, 7 (Nashville: United Methodist Publishing House, 1989), 57.

1. For more on this posture, I recommend Dan Kent's excellent book, *Confident Humility: Becoming Your Full Self Without Becoming Full of Yourself* (Minneapolis: Fortress Press, 2019).

2. Lesslie Newbigin, *Signs amid the Rubble: The Purposes of God in Human History*, ed. Geoffrey Wainwright (Grand Rapids, MI: Eerdmans, 2003), 47.

CHAPTER 9: NO THREAT TO THE THRONE

Epigraph: Maltbie Babcock, "This Is My Father's World," in *The United Methodist Hymnal: Book of United Methodist Worship*, 7 (Nashville: United Methodist Publishing House, 1989), 144.

1. John H. Walton, "Creation," in *Dictionary of the Old Testament: Pentateuch*, ed. T. Desmond Alexander and David W. Baker (Downers Grove, IL: InterVarsity Press, 2003), 161.

2. Benjamin R. Foster, "Epic of Creation (1.111) (Enuma Elish)," in *The Context of Scripture*, ed. William W. Hallo and K. Lawson Younger (Leiden: Brill, 2003), 398 (see Tablet IV, lines 102–105).

3. Robert K. Ritner, "The Repulsing of the Dragon (1.21) (Coffin Text 160)," in *The Context of Scripture*, ed. William W. Hallo and K. Lawson Younger (Leiden: Brill, 2003), 1:32.

4. Some theologians feel Genesis 1:2 starts with a cosmic battle of sorts, where "*darkness was over the surface of the deep*" depicts evil forces. This view, well explained by Dr. Leonard of Samford University, finds that "God has controlled the sea and the darkness, but he has only *controlled* these forces, not *banished* them entirely." Jeffery M. Leonard, *Creation Rediscovered: Finding New Meaning in an Ancient Story* (Peabody, MA: Hendrickson Academic, 2020), 156. I find Dr. Averbeck's rebuttal compelling: "The point of v. 2 is to provide a starting point for God's creative activity that the ancient Israelites could understand. In their ancient Near Eastern world numerous creation accounts from Mesopotamia and Egypt began with a deep dark watery abyss. In these texts this condition is seen as uncreated but *not* evil." Richard E. Averbeck, "Ancient Near Eastern Mythography as It Relates to Historiography in the Hebrew Bible: Genesis 3 and the Cosmic Battle," in *The Future of Biblical Archaeology: Reassessing Methodologies and Assumptions: The Proceedings of a Symposium, August 12–14, 2001 at Trinity International University*, ed. James Karl Hoffmeier and A. R. Millard (Grand Rapids, MI: Eerdmans, 2004), 350.

5. Walton, "Creation," 163.

6. Dr. Longman succinctly states: "There is no divine conflict because God has no rivals." Tremper Longman III, "What Genesis 1–2 Teaches

(and What It Doesn't)," in *Reading Genesis 1–2: An Evangelical Conversation*, ed. J. Daryl Charles (Peabody, MA: Hendrickson Publishers, 2013), 107.

7. Dr. Averbeck helpfully reminds us, "Genesis 3, in fact, is included in the time of creation by its readily apparent connection back to Genesis 2. There are *not* two views of creation in Genesis 1 and 2–3—just two different ways of articulating it. Both see God as the sovereign king, but only the latter expresses it in terms of cosmic battle." Averbeck, "Ancient Near Eastern Mythography as It Relates to Historiography in the Hebrew Bible: Genesis 3 and the Cosmic Battle," 354.

8. Averbeck, "Ancient Near Eastern Mythography as It Relates to Historiography in the Hebrew Bible: Genesis 3 and the Cosmic Battle," 354.

9. Revelation 12:9 tells us that Satan and the serpent are one and the same.

10. Ben Witherington, *Torah Old and New: Exegesis, Intertextuality, and Hermeneutics* (Minneapolis: 1517 Media, Fortress Press, 2018), 41.

11. Eugene Peterson takes the title of his book on discipleship from a quote by Nietzsche. Eugene H. Peterson, *Long Obedience in the Same Direction: Discipleship in an Instant Society* (Downers Grove, IL: InterVarsity Press, 2021), 11.

CHAPTER 10: SABBATH FOR RESTLESS HEARTS

Epigraph: Maltbie Babcock, "This Is My Father's World," in *The United Methodist Hymnal: Book of United Methodist Worship*, 7 (Nashville: United Methodist Publishing House, 1989), 144.

1. The Mishnah, an account of oral traditions in Judaism by rabbis during the second temple period, has thirty-nine (forty less one) restrictions for the Sabbath. The book of Jubilees, an ancient book that covers much of Genesis and is considered pseudographical by Protestants, Catholics, and others, lists twenty-two Sabbath restrictions. Sidney B. Hoenig, "The Designated Number of Kinds of Labor Prohibited on the Sabbath," *The Jewish Quarterly Review* 68, no. 4 (1978), 199.

2. James C. VanderKam, "Judaism in the Land of Israel," in *Early Judaism: A Comprehensive Overview*, ed. John J. Collins and Daniel C. Harlow (Grand Rapids, MI: Eerdmans, 2012), 81.

3. When Jesus pointed out David eating the consecrated bread, it's possible He was using their dialogue style to remind them that even their heroes skirted the letter of the law to meet their needs.

4. James C. VanderKam, "Judaism in the Land of Israel," 83.

5. 1. The man possessed by an impure spirit in the synagogue at Capernaum (Mark 1:21–28; Luke 4:31–37). 2. The paralytic at the Pool of Bethesda (John 5:1–16). 3. The blind man at the Pool of Siloam (John 9:1–16). 4. The woman crippled by a spirit for eighteen years (Luke 13:10–17). 5. The man with the abnormal swelling (Luke 14:1–6). 6. Peter's mother-in-law (Matt. 8:14–15; Mark 1:29–31; Luke 4:38–39). 7. The man with the shriveled hand (Mark 3:1–6).

DISCUSSION QUESTIONS

1. Lesslie Newbigin, *Signs amid the Rubble: The Purposes of God in Human History*, ed. Geoffrey Wainwright (Grand Rapids, MI: Eerdmans, 2003), 47.

COSMOGONY QUICK REFERENCE

1. In the introduction to his translation, Allen notes that "our understanding of Egyptian grammar and theology have now made a date in the Nineteenth Dynasty more likely." James P. Allen, "From the 'Memphite Theology' (1.15)," in *The Context of Scripture*, ed. William W. Hallo and K. Lawson Younger (Leiden: Brill, 2003), 21–22.

2. W. G. Lambert, ed., *Babylonian Creation Myths*, Mesopotamian Civilizations 16 (Winona Lake, IN: Eisenbrauns, 2013), 3.

3. Foster says in the introduction to his translation, where he provides background information on the text, "The composition is nearly complete in a Late Old Babylonian recension in three tablets (chapters) . . ." Benjamin R. Foster, "Atra-Hasis (1.130)," in *The Context of Scripture*, ed. William W. Hallo and K. Lawson Younger (Leiden: Brill, 2003), 1:450.

4. Thorkild Jacobsen, "The Eridu Genesis (1.158)," in *The Context of Scripture*, ed. William W. Hallo and K. Lawson Younger (Leiden: Brill, 2003), 1:513.

5. W. G. Lambert, ed., *Babylonian Creation Myths*, 330.

TWENTY-FIRST-CENTURY QUESTIONS

1. Alister E. McGrath, *Christian Theology: An Introduction*, 4th ed. (Malden, MA: Blackwell, 2008), 169.

2. Janet Soskice, "Why *Creatio Ex Nihilo* for Theology Today?," in *Creation Ex Nihilo: Origins, Development, Contemporary Challenges*, ed. Gary A. Anderson (Notre Dame, IN: University of Notre Dame Press, 2017), 38.

3. Soskice, "Why *Creatio Ex Nihilo* for Theology Today?," 38.

4. Tremper Longman III, *Confronting Old Testament Controversies: Pressing Questions about Evolution, Sexuality, History, and Violence* (Grand Rapids, MI: Baker Books, 2019), 40–41.

5. Longman, *Confronting Old Testament Controversies*, 41.

6. John H. Walton, *The Lost World of Genesis One: Ancient Cosmology and the Origins Debate* (Downers Grove, IL: IVP Academic, 2009), 55.

7. James P. Allen, "From Coffin Texts Spell 78 (1.7)," in *The Context of Scripture*, ed. William W. Hallo and K. Lawson Younger (Leiden: Brill, 2003), 1:11; James P. Allen, "From Coffin Texts Spell 335 = Book of the Dead Spell 17 (1.10)," in *The Context of Scripture*, ed. William W. Hallo and K. Lawson Younger (Leiden: Brill, 2003), 1:15–17.

BIBLIOGRAPHY

Allen, James P. "From Coffin Texts Spell 76 (1.6)." In *The Context of Scripture*, edited by William W. Hallo and K. Lawson Younger, 1:10–11. Leiden: Brill, 2003.

———. "From Coffin Texts Spell 78 (1.7)." In *The Context of Scripture*, edited by William W. Hallo and K. Lawson Younger, 1:11. Leiden: Brill, 2003.

———. "From Coffin Texts Spell 80 (1.8)." In *The Context of Scripture*, edited by William W. Hallo and K. Lawson Younger, 1:11–14. Leiden: Brill, 2003.

———. "From Coffin Texts Spell 335 = Book of the Dead Spell 17 (1.10)." In *The Context of Scripture*, edited by William W. Hallo and K. Lawson Younger, 1:15–17. Leiden: Brill, 2003.

———. "From Papyrus Lieden I 350 (1.16)." In *The Context of Scripture*, edited by William W. Hallo and K. Lawson Younger, 1:23–26. Leiden: Brill, 2003.

———. "From Pyramid Texts Spell 527 (1.3)." In *The Context of Scripture*, edited by William W. Hallo and K. Lawson Younger, 1:7. Leiden: Brill, 2003.

———. "From Pyramid Texts Spell 600 (1.4)." In *The Context of Scripture*, edited by William W. Hallo and K. Lawson Younger, 1:7–8. Leiden: Brill, 2003.

———. "From the 'Memphite Theology' (1.15)." In *The Context of Scripture*, edited by William W. Hallo and K. Lawson Younger, 1:21–23. Leiden: Brill, 2003.

————. "Genesis in Egypt: The Philosophy of Ancient Egyptian Creation Accounts." In *Yale Egyptological Studies 2*, Yale Egyptological Seminar: 1–114. New Haven, CT: Yale University Press, 1988.

————. *Middle Egyptian: An Introduction to the Language and Culture of Hieroglyphs*. 2nd ed. Cambridge; New York: Cambridge University Press, 2010.

Augustine. *The Confessions*. Edited by John E. Rotelle. Translated by Maria Boulding. *The Works of Saint Augustine: A Translation for the 21st Century, Part 1: Books, Volume 1*. Hyde Park, NY: New City Press, 1997.

Averbeck, Richard E. "A Literary Day, Inter-Textual, and Contextual Reading of Genesis 1–2." In *Reading Genesis 1–2: An Evangelical Conversation*, edited by J. Daryl Charles, 7–34. Peabody, MA: Hendrickson Publishers, 2013.

————. "Ancient Near Eastern Mythography as It Relates to Historiography in the Hebrew Bible: Genesis 3 and the Cosmic Battle." In *The Future of Biblical Archaeology: Reassessing Methodologies and Assumptions: The Proceedings of a Symposium, August 12–14, 2001 at Trinity International University*. Edited by James Karl Hoffmeier and A. R. Millard, 328–56. Grand Rapids, MI: Eerdmans, 2004.

————. "The Cylinders of Gudea (2.155)." In *The Context of Scripture*, edited by William W. Hallo and K. Lawson Younger, 2:417–33. Leiden: Brill, 2003.

————. "Myth, Ritual, and Order in 'Enki and the World Order,'" *Journal of the American Oriental Society* 123, no. 4, 757–71 (October–December 2003).

Babcock, Maltbie. "This Is My Father's World." In *The United Methodist Hymnal: Book of United Methodist Worship*, 7. print., 144. Nashville: United Methodist Publishing House, 1989.

Baker, Sir Richard. *Meditations and Disquisitions upon the First Psalm; The Penitential Psalms; and Seven Consolatory Psalms*. 2nd ed. London: Charles Higham, 1882.

Batto, Bernard F. *In the Beginning: Essays on Creation Motifs in the Ancient Near East and the Bible*. Siphrut: Literature and Theology of the Hebrew Scriptures 9. Winona Lake, IN: Eisenbrauns, 2013.

———. "The Sleeping God: An Ancient Near Eastern Motif of Divine Sovereignty." *Biblica* 68, no. 2 (1987): 153–77.

Beal, Todd S. "Reading Genesis 1–2: A Literal Approach." In *Reading Genesis 1–2: An Evangelical Conversation*, edited by J. Daryl Charles, 45–59. Peabody, MA: Hendrickson Publishers, 2013.

Beckman, Gary. "How Religion Was Done." In *A Companion to the Ancient Near East*. Edited by Daniel C. Snell, 343–53. Malden, MA: Blackwell, 2008.

———. "Plague Prayers of Mursili II (1.60)." In *The Context of Scripture*. Edited by William W. Hallo and K. Lawson Younger, 1:156–160. Leiden: Brill, 2003.

Charles, J. Daryl, ed. *Reading Genesis 1–2: An Evangelical Conversation*, Peabody, MA: Hendrickson Publishers, 2013.

Chisholm, Thomas O. "Great Is Thy Faithfulness." In *The United Methodist Hymnal: Book of United Methodist Worship*, 7. print, 140. Nashville: United Methodist Publishing House, 1989.

Collins, C. John. "Reading Genesis 1–2 With the Grain: Analogical Days." In *Reading Genesis 1–2: An Evangelical Conversation*. Edited by J. Daryl Charles, 73–93. Peabody, MA: Hendrickson Publishers, 2013.

Farber, Walter. "Witchcraft, Magic, and Divination in Ancient Mesopotamia." In *Civilizations of the Ancient Near East I–IV*. Edited by Jack M. Sasson, 1895–1909. New York: Scribner, 1995.

Fleming, Daniel. "The Installation of the Storm God's High Priestess (1.122)." In *The Context of Scripture*. Edited by William W. Hallo and K. Lawson Younger, 1:427–431. Leiden: Brill, 2003.

Foster, Benjamin R. "Atra-Hasis (1.130)." In *The Context of Scripture*. Edited by William W. Hallo and K. Lawson Younger, 1:450–453. Leiden: Brill, 2003.

———. "Epic of Creation (Enuma Elish) (1.111)." In *The Context of Scripture*. Edited by William W. Hallo and K. Lawson Younger, 1:390–402. Leiden: Brill, 2003.

———. "The Poem of the Righteous Sufferer (1.153)." In *The Context of Scripture*. Edited by William W. Hallo and K. Lawson Younger, 1:486–492. Leiden: Brill, 2003.

Fox, Michael V. "Papyrus Chester Beatty I (1.51)." In *The Context of Scripture*. Edited by William W. Hallo and K. Lawson Younger, 1:128–130. Leiden: Brill, 2003.

Greig, Pete. *How to Pray: A Simple Guide for Normal People*. Colorado Springs, CO: NavPress, 2019.

Hoenig, Sidney B. "The Designated Number of Kinds of Labor Prohibited on the Sabbath." *The Jewish Quarterly Review* 68, no. 4 (1978): 193–208.

Hoffmeier, James K. "Some Thoughts on Genesis 1 & 2 and Egyptian Cosmology." *The Journal of the Ancient Near Eastern Society* 15 (1983): 39–49.

Horowitz, Wayne, Takayoshi Oshima, and Seth Sanders. *Cuneiform in Canaan: Cuneiform Sources from the Land of Israel in Ancient Times*. Jerusalem: Israel Exploration Society, 2006.

Hundley, Michael. *Yahweh Among the Gods: The Divine in Genesis, Exodus, and the Ancient Near East*. Cambridge: Cambridge University Press, 2022.

Jacobsen, Thorkild. "The Eridu Genesis (1.158)." In *The Context of Scripture*. Edited by William W. Hallo and K. Lawson Younger, 1:513–515. Leiden: Brill, 2003.

Kent, Dan. *Confident Humility: Becoming Your Full Self Without Becoming Full of Yourself*. Minneapolis: Fortress Press, 2019.

Klein, Jacob. "Enki and Ninmah." In *The Context of Scripture*. Edited by William W. Hallo and K. Lawson Younger, 1:516–18. Leiden: Brill, 2003.

Koehler, Ludwig and Walter Baumgartner, eds. "רקיע." In *The Hebrew and Aramaic Lexicon of the Old Testament: Study Edition*. Leiden: Brill, 2001.

Lambert, W. G., ed. *Babylonian Creation Myths*. Mesopotamian Civilizations 16. Winona Lake, IN: Eisenbrauns, 2013.

Leonard, Jeffery M. *Creation Rediscovered: Finding New Meaning in an Ancient Story*. Peabody, MA: Hendrickson Academic, 2020.

Levenson, Jon D. "The Temple and the World." *The Journal of Religion* 64, no. 3 (1984): 275–98.

Lichtheim, Miriam. "Merikare (1.35)." In *The Context of Scripture*. Edited by William W. Hallo and K. Lawson Younger, 1:61–66. Leiden: Brill, 2003.

Longman III, Tremper. *Confronting Old Testament Controversies: Pressing Questions about Evolution, Sexuality, History, and Violence*. Grand Rapids, MI: Baker Books, 2019. Accessed January 20, 2024. ProQuest Ebook Central.

———. "What Genesis 1–2 Teaches (and What It Doesn't)." In *Reading Genesis 1–2: An Evangelical Conversation*. Edited by J. Daryl Charles, 103–28. Peabody, MA: Hendrickson Publishers, 2013.

Lucas, E. C. "Cosmology." In *Dictionary of the Old Testament: Pentateuch*. Edited by T. Desmond Alexander and David W. Baker, 130–39. Downers Grove, IL: InterVarsity Press, 2003.

McDowell, Catherine L. *The Image of God in the Garden of Eden: The Creation of Humankind in Genesis 2:5–3:24 in Light of the Mīs Pî Pīt Pî and Wpt-r Rituals of Mesopotamia and Ancient Egypt*. Siphrut: Literature and Theology of the Hebrew Scriptures 15. Winona Lake, IN: Eisenbrauns, 2015.

McGrath, Alister E. *Christian Theology: An Introduction*. 4th. ed. Malden, MA: Blackwell, 2008.

Middleton, J. Richard. *The Liberating Image: The Imago Dei in Genesis 1*. Grand Rapids, MI: Brazos Press, 2005.

Newbigin, Lesslie. *Signs amid the Rubble: The Purposes of God in Human History*. Edited by Geoffrey Wainwright. Grand Rapids, MI: Eerdmans, 2003.

Pardee, Dennis. "The Ba'lu Myth (1.86)." In *The Context of Scripture*. Edited by William W. Hallo and K. Lawson Younger, 2:241–274. Leiden: Brill, 2003.

Peterson, Eugene H. *A Long Obedience in the Same Direction: Discipleship in an Instant Society*. Downers Grove, IL: InterVarsity Press, 2021.

Polonsky, Janice. "The Rise of the Sun God and the Determination of Destiny in Ancient Mesopotamia." PhD, University of Pennsylvania, 2002.

Richter, Sandra L. *The Epic of Eden: A Christian Entry into the Old Testament*. Downers Grove, IL: IVP Academic, 2008.

Ritner, Robert K. "The Repulsing of the Dragon (1.21) (Coffin Text 160)." In *The Context of Scripture*, edited by William W. Hallo and K. Lawson Younger, 1:32. Leiden: Brill, 2003.

Sarna, Nahum M. *Exploring Exodus: The Heritage of Biblical Israel*. New York: Schocken Books, 1986.

Schloen, J. David. *The House of the Father as Fact and Symbol: Patrimonialism in Ugarit and the Ancient Near East*. Studies in the Archaeology and History of the Levant 2. Winona Lake, IN: Eisenbrauns, 2001.

Smith, Mark S. *The Origins of Biblical Monotheism: Israel's Polytheistic Background and the Ugaritic Texts*. New York: Oxford University Press, 2001.

———. *The Priestly Vision of Genesis 1*. Minneapolis: Fortress Press, 2010.

Smith, Rachel Booth. "If Troubled, Look for God's Comfort. If Restless, Look for His Lordship." *Christianity Today*, December 2022.

Soskice, Janet. "Why *Creatio Ex Nihilo* for Theology Today?" In *Creation Ex Nihilo: Origins, Development, Contemporary Challenges*. Edited by Gary A. Anderson, 37–54. Notre Dame, IN: University of Notre Dame Press, 2017.

Spafford, Horatio G. "It Is Well with My Soul." In *The United Methodist Hymnal: Book of United Methodist Worship*, 7. Nashville: United Methodist Publishing House, 1989.

te Velde, Herman. "Theology, Priests, and Worship in Ancient Egypt." In *Civilizations of the Ancient Near East I–IV*. Edited by Jack M. Sasson, 1731–1749. New York: Scribner, 1995. Van De Mieroop, Marc. *A History of the Ancient Near East ca. 3000–323 BC*. 3rd ed. Blackwell History of the Ancient World. Chichester, West Sussex, UK: Wiley Blackwell, 2016.

Van De Mieroop, Marc. *A History of the Ancient Near East ca. 3000–323 BC*. 3rd ed. Blackwell History of the Ancient World. Chichester, West Sussex, UK: Wiley Blackwell, 2016.

VanderKam, James C. "Judaism in the Land of Israel." In *Early Judaism: A Comprehensive Overview*. Edited by John J. Collins and Daniel C. Harlow, 70–94. Grand Rapids, MI: Eerdmans, 2012.

Walton, John H. *Ancient Near Eastern Thought and the Old Testament: Introducing the Conceptual World of the Hebrew Bible*. 2nd ed. Grand Rapids, MI: Baker Academic, 2018.

———. "Creation." In *Dictionary of the Old Testament: Pentateuch*. Edited by T. Desmond Alexander and David W. Baker, 155–68. Downers Grove, IL: InterVarsity Press, 2003.

———. *Genesis 1 as Ancient Cosmology*. Winona Lake, IN: Eisenbrauns, 2011.

———. *Genesis: From Biblical Text . . . to Contemporary Life*. The NIV Application Commentary. Grand Rapids, MI: Zondervan, 2001.

———. "Interpreting the Bible as an Ancient Near Eastern Document." In *Israel: Ancient Kingdom or Late Invention?* Edited by Daniel I. Block, 304–32. Nashville: B&H Academic Group, 2008.

———. "Reading Genesis 1 as Ancient Cosmology." In *Reading Genesis 1–2: An Evangelical Conversation*. Edited by J. Daryl Charles, 141–69. Peabody, MA: Hendrickson Publishers, 2013.

———. *The Lost World of Genesis One: Ancient Cosmology and the Origins Debate*. Downers Grove, IL: IVP Academic, 2009.

Wenham, Gordon J. *Exploring the Old Testament: A Guide to the Pentateuch*. Exploring the Bible Series, Vol. 1. Downers Grove, IL: InterVarsity Press, 2008.

———. *Genesis 1–15*. Word Biblical Commentary. Waco, TX: Word Books, 1987.

Witherington, Ben. *Torah Old and New: Exegesis, Intertextuality, and Hermeneutics*. Minneapolis: 1517 Media, Fortress Press, 2018.

Wesley, Charles. "O for a Thousand Tongues to Sing." In *The United Methodist Hymnal: Book of United Methodist Worship*, 7. print, 57. Nashville: United Methodist Publishing House, 1989.

Wright, Tom. *The Lord and His Prayer*. Great Britain: BPC Paperbacks Ltd., 1996.

You finished reading!

Did this book help you in some way? If so, please consider writing an honest review wherever you purchase your books. Your review gets this book into the hands of more readers and helps us continue to create biblically faithful resources.

Moody Publishers books help fund the training of students for ministry around the world.

The **Moody Bible Institute** is one of the most well-known Christian institutions in the world, training thousands of young people to faithfully serve Christ wherever He calls them. And when you buy and read a book from Moody Publishers, you're helping make that vital ministry training possible.

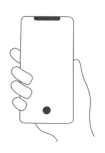

Continue to dive into the Word, *anytime, anywhere.*

Find what you need to take your next step in your walk with Christ: from uplifting music to sound preaching, our programs are designed to help you right when you need it.

Download the **Moody Radio App** and start listening today!

 MOODY
Publishers®

 MOODY
Bible Institute™

 MOODY
Radio™